ESS, JULY 4, 1776.

hirteen united States of America,

n one people to dissolve the political bands which have connected them with another, and to

Nature's God entitle them, a decent respect to the opinions of mankind requires that they

aths to be self-evident, that all men are created equal, that they are endowed by their Creator

— That to secure these rights, Governments are instituted among Men, deriving their just

of these ends, it is the Right of the People to alter or to abolish it, and to institute new

o them shall seem most likely to effect their Safety and Happiness. Prudence, indeed,

nd accordingly all experience hath shewn, that mankind are more disposed to suffer, while

Bat when a long train of abuses and usurpations, pursuing invariably the same Object

such Government, and to provide new Guards for their future security. — Such has

ice their former Systems of Government. The history of the present King of Great

an absolute Tyranny over these States. To prove this, let Facts be submitted to a candid

the public good. ——— He has forbidden his Governors to pass Laws of immediate

when so suspended, he has utterly neglected to attend to them ——— He has refused to

e right of Representation in the Legislature, a right inestimable to them and formidable

distant from the depository of their Public Records, for the sole purpose of fatiguing them into

g with manly firmness his invasions on the rights of the people. ——— He has refused for

e of Annihilation, have returned to the People at large for their exercise; the State remain

——— He has endeavoured to prevent the Population of these States; for that purpose obstruc

and raising the conditions of new Appropriations of Lands. ——— He has obstructed the

has made Judges dependent on his Will alone, for the tenure of their offices, and the amount

ms of Officers to harass our people, and eat out their substance ——— He has kept among

nder the Military independent of and superior to the Civil power? ——— He has combined

iving his Assent to their Acts of pretended Legislation: ——— For Quartering large bodies of

MASTER GEORGE'S PEOPLE

GEORGE WASHINGTON, HIS SLAVES, AND HIS REVOLUTIONARY TRANSFORMATION

BY MARFÉ FERGUSON DELANO WITH MOUNT VERNON

PHOTOGRAPHY BY LORI EPSTEIN

NATIONAL GEOGRAPHIC

WASHINGTON, D.C.

When this image of Mount Vernon was painted, some of Washington's enslaved workers lived in the two-story building to the right of the white fence. Called the House for Families, it was later demolished and the slaves moved into new quarters attached to the greenhouse.

The Slave Memorial at Mount Vernon was designed and built in 1983 by Howard University architecture students. The granite column sits on top of three circles engraved with the words faith, hope, and love. It is adjacent to a 1929 Mount Vernon Ladies' Association marker noting the site of the slave burial ground. About 75 individuals are buried here, but no grave markers survive to identify them. A ceremony honoring the enslaved people who once lived and worked at Mount Vernon takes place at the site every year with Black Women United for Action.

ACKNOWLEDGMENTS

Many thanks to Mary V. Thompson, a good neighbor who also happens to be a research historian at Mount Vernon, for generously sharing her own research and for her expert review of this book. Thanks also to Mount Vernon's Jim Rees, Jamie Bosket, Joan Stahl, and especially to Melissa Wood for coordinating our photo shoots at the estate. Very special thanks to Caroline Christensen, Nicolette Christensen, Amaris Makena Greene, and Atira Maisha Greene, young students who make their debut as historical interpreters in this book. They were a joy to work with, as were Mount Vernon's stellar staff interpreters Azie Mira Dungey, Mary Wiseman, Peter Curtis, Jonathan Douglass, and Tom Plott.

I am grateful to Professor Edna Greene Medford of Howard University for her expert review of this book, to ZSun-nee Matema for her moving endnote, and to Ruth Williams for our tête-à-têtes. I thank my writing group—Jackie, Marty, Suzy, Moira, Liz, Madelyn, Anamaria, Martha, Carla, Anna, and Wendy—for their input on early drafts of several chapters. My research got under way during a residential fellowship at the Virginia Center for Creative Arts, which was underwritten in part by the Morris and Gwendolyn Cafritz Foundation. My deep appreciation goes to both organizations. And to my amazingly talented and creative National Geographic colleagues Jennifer Emmett, Lori Epstein, and Jim Hiscott, I thank you for your belief in this book, and in me.

CONTENTS

"DO NOT **SUFFER** THE QUARTER NEGRO CHILDREN TO BE IN THE KITCHEN, OR IN THE YARDS UNLESS BROUGHT THERE ON **BUSINESS**— AS BESIDES THE BAD HABIT—THEY TOO FREQUENTLY ARE BREAKING LIMBS, OR TWIGS FROM, OR DOING OTHER **INJURY** TO MY SHRUBS."

Letter of George Washington to William Pearce, 22 December 1793

CHAPTER 1

A SHORT-LIVED CHILDHOOD

L IKE CHILDREN EVERYWHERE, the enslaved girls and boys who lived on President George Washington's Virginia plantation, Mount Vernon, liked to play together. While their parents cleaned Washington's mansion house or cooked his family's meals or groomed his horses or toiled in his fields from dawn to dusk, the slave children seem to have looked after themselves. And as children will do, they sometimes played where they had been told not to.

When Washington's new farm manager, William Pearce, arrived at Mount Vernon in the fall of 1793, he was dismayed to see that the slave children had the run of the grounds. "I thought I saw a great many at your mansion house," he wrote to his employer.

At the time Washington himself was in Philadelphia, leading the new nation he had helped create. He answered Pearce's letter promptly, as he usually did with matters concerning Mount Vernon. He had loved it ever since he was a boy. No matter how far away he was from Mount Vernon, it was never far from his thoughts.

He already knew that the children played around his mansion. They had been doing it for years. "There are a great number of Negro children at the quarters belonging to the house people," he replied to Pearce.

George Washington often called the enslaved human beings he owned his "people." The "house people" worked as personal servants to the Washington family. They were the maids and butlers and waiters, the seamstresses and grooms. Most of them lived close to

On the shores of the Potomac River, a boy and girl portray 18th-century enslaved children at George Washington's Mount Vernon Estate. Historical interpreters—trained role players—reenact slave life throughout this book.
⚭

In the greenhouse slave quarters, an interpreter works on an animal trap similar to ones that slaves would have used in colonial times to catch rabbits. Ten to 20 male slaves shared the men's bunk room. The women's bunk room, on the other side of the greenhouse, housed about a dozen female slaves and perhaps their children. Most of the people who lived in these quarters were house servants or skilled workers. Some were single, while others had families living elsewhere.

the mansion house, either in their own tiny cabins or above the outbuildings or in a dormitory-style building known as the quarters.

"But," continued Washington, the children "have always been forbid (except two or three young ones belonging to the cook . . .) from coming within the gates of the enclosures of the yards, gardens, etc." The cook's name was Lucy. Her husband, Frank Lee, was a house servant and waiter. Their children—who included Phil, Patty, and Burwell—were the only ones with permission to play near the mansion.

As Washington admitted to Pearce, however, the rest of the children "are often in there notwithstanding." Something about the area was irresistible. Perhaps it was the long lawn in front of the mansion, compared by a French visitor to "a playground carpeted in green." The walled gardens on either side of the lawn must have been especially tempting. It's easy to imagine children racing around the gravel paths, leaping over shrubs and swinging from trees. During the fun a twig might snap or a branch break off and get used as a pretend sword. Careless feet might trample vegetables or flowers. And who could resist picking a juicy apple or pear when the ripe fruit dangled from the trees?

Among the young trespassers might have been Wilson, Rachel, and Jemima. Their mother, Caroline, served as a maid in the mansion house. Timothy and Elvey might

have played there too. Their mother, Charlotte, was a seamstress who sometimes worked in the mansion.

Washington told Pearce why the slave children were banned from the area. It was so "they may not be breaking the shrubs, and doing other mischief." Washington took great pride in Mount Vernon's gardens. He had designed them himself, and he enjoyed showing them off to guests. He was especially proud of the boxwood shrubs arranged in an elegant shape known as a fleur-de-lis.

But aside from his complaints, Washington seems to have done little to stop the children from playing there. As President, he no doubt had more important things on his mind. And perhaps he didn't have the heart to enforce the ban. He knew that the enslaved children would soon be put to work for him, when they were between 11 and 14 years old. About this, he was quite clear: "So soon as they are able to work out I expect to reap the benefit of their labor myself." In this time, it was not unusual for enslaved children—or free children, for that matter—to start work at such an early age. The difference was that if you were a free child, your parents decided when and where you would be put to work. If you were an enslaved child, your owner decided your fate.

George Washington became a slave owner when he was only a boy himself. When

As enslaved children at Mount Vernon might have done, young reenactors play tag in the boxwood garden near the mansion house. Washington grumbled more than once about Negro children "breaking limbs, or twigs from, or doing other injury to my shrubs." The long, low building behind the garden is a reconstruction of the slave quarters attached to the greenhouse. The entrance is on the opposite side, which would have been out of view of Washington's guests.

his father, Augustine Washington, died in 1743, he left 11-year-old George ten enslaved workers. George also inherited the family home, a plantation called Ferry Farm near Fredericksburg, Virginia.

Young George took slavery for granted. He had grown up watching his father's slaves tend the farm animals, clear the fields, and plant, hoe, and harvest the crops. Other slaves cooked, cleaned, and washed clothes for the Washington family. They helped care for the Washington children. George's neighbors and older half-brothers also owned slaves.

African people were first sold as servants in Virginia in 1619. Over the next two centuries, many thousands more African men, women, and children were captured, shipped across the Atlantic Ocean to the Americas, and sold to colonists to be unpaid workers for the rest of their lives. By the time George Washington was born in 1732, slavery was a fact of life in American society. Enslaved black people were considered a "species of property," just like horses or dogs or tables or chairs. They could be bought, sold, rented, traded, or given away as gifts. They had no rights at all. Today it is difficult for us to understand this attitude, but in the 1700s many people saw things differently. Very few white colonists objected to slavery. And the slaves themselves had no say in the matter.

FRANK LEE

AFTER SERVING as an enslaved waiter at Mount Vernon for many years, Frank Lee worked his way up to the prestigious job of butler. His wife, Lucy, cooked for the Washingtons and their guests. For a while, the couple and their children lived in two rooms above the kitchen.

Frank Lee saw to it that his master's dining table was properly set for meals. He supervised the waiters who served the food at the table. Many years later one of Washington's guests recalled, "The dishes and plate were removed and changed, with a silence and speed that seemed like enchantment."

As butler, Frank was expected to "make all the others [household servants] do their duty properly." He oversaw the cleaning of the mansion at least once a week. He made sure the Washingtons' linens, china, silver, and glassware were cleaned and stored properly. Frank kept tabs on the ice supply in the icehouse in the summer and gathered black walnuts—one of Washington's favorite foods—during the fall. George Washington also entrusted Frank with the care and breeding of his hunting dogs.

Frank Lee seems to have had a warm and welcoming personality. One visitor to Mount Vernon praised his "politeness and kindness." Martha Washington's grandson described him as the "most polite and accomplished of all butlers." But while George Washington was away from Mount Vernon during his Presidency, he worried that Frank might be "ruined by idleness." And so Frank was given other jobs, including painting the mansion house, helping the gardener with the hedges and lawns, digging brick clay, and shoveling gravel. Used to serving in the house, Frank may have chafed at being assigned to physical labor. But as an enslaved person, he was not given a choice.

Sketched by a visitor to Mount Vernon in 1796, this scene shows Martha Washington, seated, preparing tea on the terrace. The man behind her may be Frank Lee, the butler. Standing at left is Martha's granddaughter, Nelly Custis. Sitting on the ground is a young house guest.

"LET THERE BE TWO THIRDS OF THEM **MALES**, THE OTHER THIRD **FEMALES** . . . ALL OF THEM TO BE STRAIGHT LIMBED . . . WITH **GOOD TEETH** AND GOOD COUNTENANCES."

Letter of George Washington to Daniel Jenifer Adams, 20 July 1772

CHAPTER 2

BUILDING A PLANTATION

LEFT: *Washington required his enslaved waiters, butlers, and footmen to wear formal uniforms, called livery, similar to the one worn by this historical interpreter.*

BOTTOM: *At age 16, George Washington made his first trip to the Virginia frontier to survey land.*

ALTHOUGH GEORGE WASHINGTON became the owner of ten human beings at age 11, he was too young to take charge of them then. His mother, Mary Ball Washington, managed Ferry Farm and oversaw his slaves for him. Meanwhile George's older half-brother, Lawrence Washington, helped raise him. They spent a great deal of time together at Mount Vernon, which at the time was Lawrence's home.

As a teenager George worked as a surveyor, measuring and mapping the wilds of western Virginia. In his 20s, he served as an officer in the colonial militia and became widely known as a brave and gifted leader. At age 26, George retired from military service to take up the life of a gentleman farmer at Mount Vernon. He was now master of the Potomac River plantation and its enslaved men, women, and children. The estate had been left to him by Lawrence, who had died a few years earlier.

George Washington was ambitious. He wanted to turn Mount Vernon into a top-notch plantation, become very rich, and make a name for himself in Virginia's powerful upper class. To achieve these goals, he needed more land and more slaves to work that land. He borrowed money to buy both. By 1758, he had about 40 enslaved laborers at Mount Vernon. This included a crew of carpenters, who stayed busy that year renovating Lawrence's modest farmhouse. Washington was ready to take a wife, and he wanted a grand home, a mansion, for her.

In January 1759, George Washington married Martha Dandridge Custis, a young

This portrait of Patsy and Jacky Custis was painted in 1757, two years before their mother, Martha Dandridge Custis, married George Washington. George and Martha had no children together.

widow from southern Virginia. Overnight he became a very rich man indeed. Martha's first husband, Daniel Parke Custis, had been one of the wealthiest men in Virginia. When he died, Martha received a third of his property, which included about 85 enslaved human beings. The rest of his estate went to his children, John Parke Custis (Jacky) and Martha Parke Custis (Patsy). By law, Washington gained immediate control of Martha's share of the Custis estate, called the "dower" share, when they wed. He also took charge of his stepchildren's financial affairs.

When Martha and her children moved to Mount Vernon, she brought about a dozen of her slaves with her to help set up housekeeping. Among them were a cook named Doll, a seamstress named Betty and her baby son, Austin, and a 15-year-old maid named Sally, who tended to Martha's personal needs. She helped her mistress dress, for example, and arranged her hair.

Four-year-old Jacky and three-year-old Patsy came with their own personal slaves. A ten-year-old boy named Julius waited on Jacky. Twelve-year-old Rose was Patsy's maid. A 19-year-old named Moll looked after all four of the children, white and black, and she also did their sewing. Having so many familiar faces around must have helped little Jacky and Patsy feel comfortable in their new home. And of course they had their mother. Things were different for Rose and Julius. When they climbed aboard the wagons bound for Mount Vernon, a four-day journey to the north, they probably left their own families behind forever.

At this stage of his life, Washington wasn't troubled about breaking up slave families, despite the misery it caused. His upbringing had taught him that slaves were just another type of property, valuable tools to be used as he saw fit to work his fields, increase his wealth, and contribute to his comfort. He didn't question whether slavery was right or wrong.

Over the next 16 years Washington served several terms in Virginia's colonial legislature, but building Mount Vernon into a prosperous enterprise was his main focus. During this time he purchased more than 60 new slaves. He bought them from his relatives and neighbors and

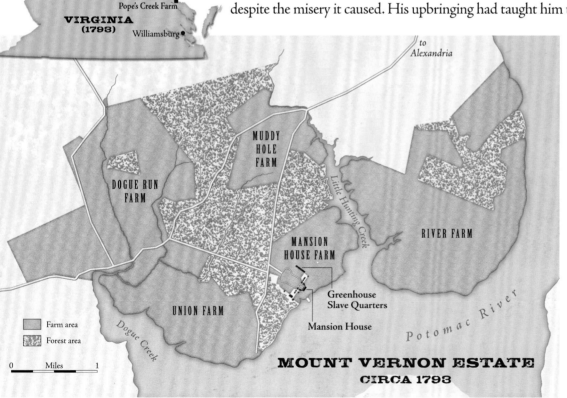

VIRGINIA (1793)

Alexandria
Mount Vernon Estate
Ferry Farm
Pope's Creek Farm
Williamsburg

to Alexandria

MUDDY HOLE FARM

DOGUE RUN FARM

RIVER FARM

Little Hunting Creek

MANSION HOUSE FARM

Greenhouse
Slave Quarters

Mansion House

UNION FARM

Dogue Creek

Potomac River

Farm area
Forest area

0   Miles   1

MOUNT VERNON ESTATE
CIRCA 1793

from slave merchants. In 1768 he acquired teenage brothers William and Frank Lee at an estate sale after the death of their master. He paid 61 pounds for William and 50 pounds for Frank. In his account book, Washington described the brothers as "mulatto," the term used to describe lighter skinned, mixed-race slaves. At the same sale, Washington also acquired a "Negro boy Adam" and another dark-skinned boy named Jack for only 19 pounds each. Like many slaveholders, Washington was willing to pay more for light-skinned people because they were considered a kind of status symbol, a sign of wealth and power. He made William his personal servant, or valet. Frank became a house servant. Dark-skinned Adam and Jack were sent to work in the fields.

Sometimes Washington looked to buy slaves with specific skills, such as carpentry experience. Other times he bargained for people like he might for livestock. In 1772, for example, he shipped 273 barrels of Mount Vernon's flour to the West Indies, with instructions that the money from the sale be "laid out in Negroes, if choice ones can be had." He described just what he wanted: "Let there be two thirds of them Males, the other third Females—the former not exceeding (at any rate) 20 years of age—the latter 16—All of them to be straight limbed, and in every respect strong and likely, with good teeth and good countenances." By buying teenagers, Washington was investing in Mount Vernon's future. Not only

Martha Washington supervised the enslaved cooks, waiters, maids, and other household staff. She also oversaw the work of the seamstresses and dairy-maids. This portrait depicts her as she might have looked at age 25, a couple of years before she married George Washington.

Sitting in the doorway of an outbuilding at Mount Vernon, an enslaved man takes a break from work in this painting by Eastman Johnson, a 19th-century artist known for his portrayals of African-American slave life. A child stands nearby in the grass, and other slaves can be seen under the breezeway connected to the mansion house.

would they be able to work for decades to come, but they also had many years of child-bearing ahead of them. And just as the lambs born to his sheep belonged to Washington by law, so did the children born to his female slaves.

Washington not only bought enslaved people during these years, he also sold some when he needed cash. And when a "healthy, strong" slave named Tom ran away one too many times, Washington shipped him off to the West Indies. He instructed the ship captain to sell Tom "for whatever he will fetch" and to bring in return for him one cask each of the best molasses and rum, along with a barrel of limes and a few other luxuries. He advised the skipper to keep Tom "handcuffed till you get to sea" and predicted he would "sell well, if kept clean and trimmed up a little."

Everyone knew that being sold to the West Indies was basically a death sentence. Laborers were forced to work so hard in the hot and steamy sugarcane fields that few lasted more than a couple of years. Nonetheless, getting rid of unruly slaves this way was a common practice on Virginia plantations. And at this time of his life, George Washington was just another ambitious plantation owner. Like most of his peers, he turned a blind eye to the evils of slavery. One time he even helped organize a lottery to raffle off human beings.

The goal of the lottery was to raise money to pay off the debts of a man named Bernard Moore. Washington participated because Moore owed his stepchildren a large sum. It was a festive affair, held in April 1769 at a tavern in Williamsburg, Virginia's colonial capital. For ten pounds, gamblers could buy a chance to win valuable prizes, including Moore's slaves. The slaves were divided into 39 groups, or lots. Several of the people being raffled off were children. Some of them were being separated from their parents. For example, one lot offered Robin, "a good Sawyer," and his wife, Bella. The next lot advertised "A Negro Girl named Sukey, about 12 years old, and another named Betty, about 7 years old, Children of Robin and Bella."

Some biographers believe that George Washington reached a moral low point with the raffle of children in Williamsburg. Fortunately, he never repeated such a vile act.

Over the years, resistance to British rule grew in the thirteen American colonies. Washington was one of the Virginia patriots who spoke out against unfair British demands and taxes. In 1775 colonial leaders chose him to command the American forces in the fight for independence.

During the Revolutionary War—and again during the eight years of his Presidency—Washington directed Mount Vernon from afar. He hired a number of different farm managers to look after it in his absence. Each week he sent them a letter filled with questions and instructions. He required them to respond with weekly "farm reports" giving details of the tasks accomplished by the slaves. He also wanted to know which people were sick or injured or had given birth or died. This correspondence, along with Washington's diaries and financial account books, tells us much of what we know about the lives of his enslaved people. The slaves themselves left no written accounts that we know of. Very few of them could read or write.

More than half of Mount Vernon's enslaved field workers were women, and they did some of the hardest and dirtiest chores. They cleaned out the stables, loaded manure in carts and spread it in the fields, and pulled tree stumps out of swamps and meadows. Washington expected his slaves to work from sunup to sundown, six days a week. In their limited leisure time, the people tended to their own small garden patches near their quarters, a scene reenacted in the picture below.

As Washington informed one farm manager, he expected "that my people . . . be at their work as soon as it is light, work 'till it is dark, and be diligent while they are at it." When he was home at Mount Vernon, he himself rose before dawn every morning and worked at his desk for a couple of hours before riding out to inspect his fields, fences, and workers. There was a lot of ground to cover. Over time Washington expanded Mount Vernon to 8,000 acres, which he divided into five separate

farms. Each of these farms had its own overseer and community of enslaved men, women, and children. Washington's home farm was called Mansion House Farm, or "Home House."

Many of the slaves who lived at the Mansion House Farm were artisans, or skilled workers. This group included carpenters, bricklayers, blacksmiths, and coopers (barrel makers). Other skilled slaves worked in food-related jobs as cooks, millers, gardeners, and dairymaids. Enslaved spinners, weavers, knitters, seamstresses, and shoemakers made the clothing that was worn by other slaves on the estate. The enslaved servants who waited on the Washingtons and their guests also lived at the Mansion House Farm. They were often of mixed race, like William and Frank Lee. A French visitor to Mount Vernon recorded that "the general's house servants are mulattoes . . . I noticed one small boy whose hair and skin were so like our own that if I had not been told, I should never have suspected his ancestry. He is nevertheless a slave for the rest of his life."

The majority of Washington's "people" lived on the outlying farms. Like the slaves on other Virginia plantations, they spent most of their lives at backbreaking labor in the fields. Work did not stop when winter came. One year it was so cold that Washington described Mount

TOP: *Flanked by stables and corn cribs, this replica of the 16-sided treading barn built by Washington's enslaved carpenters in the 1790s is based on his hand-drawn plans.*

BOTTOM: *Inside the barn, an interpreter drives horses around a wooden track spread with wheat. As the horses tread on the stalks, the grain is separated and falls through the spaces between the floorboards to the level below, where it is collected and stored.*

Vernon as "locked fast by ice," but he noted in his diary that on one farm, "the women were taking up and thinning the trees in the swamp."

This casual mention of grueling labor in an icy swamp may seem hard-hearted to us, but to Washington it was simply business as usual. Such work was necessary to make Mount Vernon productive and profitable, and he considered it his slaves' duty to do that work. His duty as their master was "to feed and clothe them well and be careful of them in sickness." In return, he wrote, "I expect such labor as they ought to render." To him it seemed a fair exchange.

Once a year, usually in the fall, Washington issued new blankets to his enslaved people. He expected them to be used for farm chores as well as for keeping warm. One winter, for example, he ordered that his "people, with their blankets, go every evening . . . to the nearest wood and fill them with leaves" to line the beds of the livestock. This was to be done, he said, so the cattle and hogs would "lay warm and comfortable." To Washington, this seemed "of great utility in every point of view." We can only imagine the point of view of the men and women who had no choice but to use their one blanket a year for such a grubby task.

DAVY

DAVY, AN ENSLAVED overseer, earned his master's respect for performing "his business as well as the white overseers, and with more quietness than any of them." Both hired white men and enslaved black men supervised the field hands at Mount Vernon's outlying farms. George Washington had a low opinion of most of them, white or black. He grumbled about their "insufferable conduct" and "inattention and carelessness." He worried that most of his hired overseers "seem to consider a Negro much in the same light as they do the brute beasts, on the farms; and often times treat them as inhumanly." Davy, on the other hand, "knows the state of his own farm" and did "very well" with "proper directions."

Washington did have one complaint about Davy. He feared the overseer was "negligent" when it came to keeping track of the livestock. "Davy's lost lambs carry with them a very suspicious appearance," he grumbled. It's likely that Davy looked the other way when lambs disappeared from the flock and ended up on slave tables. Once he told his master that "his people" weren't receiving a sufficient ration of cornmeal, and that "several of

them would often be without a mouthful for a day ... sometimes two days, before they were served again." In response, Washington asked his farm manager to make sure that "my Negroes" were given enough cornmeal "to feed them plentifully."

Davy worked as an overseer at Mount Vernon for many years. In that role, he enjoyed some special privileges, including yearly portions of pork and weekly rations of rum. He and his wife, Molly, had their own quarters. A house they lived in at one time was so ramshackle, however, that Washington's estate manager feared "that house of [Davy's] will fall if a high wind should happen and that if that should be the case and any of the family [are] in it, it may cost them their lives." Washington agreed it was dangerous, and an empty house was moved from another farm to replace the one at Muddy Hole Farm in which Davy was then living.

George Washington considered an enslaved African-American man named Davy—represented here by an interpreter—one of his best overseers. He did complain, however, about lambs and other livestock disappearing under Davy's watch.

"YOUR **MOTHER** HAS WROTE TO ME TO SEND SILLA DOWN TO HER—WHICH I SHALL DO—BUT AM VERY SORRY TO PART HER FROM JACK. HE **CRIES** AND BEGS, SAYING HE HAD RATHER BE **HANGED** THAN SEPARATED."

Letter of Lund Washington to
George Washington, 4 March 1778

CHAPTER 3

PRIVATE LIVES

An enslaved mother and her small children sit before the large fireplace in a Mount Vernon outbuilding in this painting by Eastman Johnson. When Martha Washington married George in 1759, she brought a cook named Doll to Mount Vernon with her. Years later, Doll's daughter Lucy cooked for the Washingtons.

AFTER WORKING SUNUP TO SUNDOWN Monday through Saturday for their master, the enslaved men and women at Mount Vernon got Sunday off. They also received a day off at Easter and a couple of other holidays, and four days at Christmas. They must have looked forward to this time to themselves. Of course, someone still had to milk the cows and feed and water the livestock on those days. And the cooks, butlers, waiters, and personal servants at the mansion house still had to wait on the Washington family and their guests for at least part of the day, holiday or not. But on the whole, slaves at Mount Vernon were allowed to spend their evening hours and days off as they wished. Many of them used this time to visit their friends and families.

Family ties were as important to the enslaved individuals at Mount Vernon as they are to us today. The majority of adult slaves were married. While these marriages were not recognized by Virginia law, they were honored by the slave community and by George Washington, too.

Although he had torn apart families without qualms during the first decade of his own marriage, by the mid-1770s Washington promised not to sell slaves if it meant separating husbands from wives or children from their parents. It seems he could no longer ignore how deeply attached enslaved people were to their loved ones. He was reminded of the strength of these bonds at least once during the Revolution, when his cousin Lund Washington was managing Mount Vernon for him. Mary Ball

Washington, George's mother, had asked that a Mount Vernon slave woman named Silla be sent to her down in Fredericksburg. Silla was married to Jack, a cooper. Lund wrote George that Silla would probably not want to leave Jack, because "they appear to live comfortable together." Two weeks later Lund reported that he was "very sorry to part her from Jack. He cries and begs, saying he had rather be hanged than separated." Lund finally did send Silla to Fredericksburg, but it appears the move was not permanent. About a year later Washington instructed Lund that, "In order to gratify Jack you may bring Silla up again."

Kitty and Isaac were a married couple who lived together at the Mansion House Farm for many years. Kitty worked as a spinner and a dairymaid, and Isaac was the head carpenter on the plantation. They had nine daughters: Sinah, Mima, Ally, Lucy, Grace, Letty, Nancy, Barbara, and Levina. Sinah, the oldest, married a slave named Ben, who was one of Washington's millers. Like her mother, she helped in the dairy, where Washington suspected she "never failed to take a pretty ample toll of both milk and butter." Sinah's daughter—Kitty and Isaac's granddaughter—was named Nancy, perhaps after her aunt. Enslaved children at Mount Vernon were often named after relatives, just as many children today are given family names.

An expert seamstress, Martha Washington taught enslaved girls how to sew the clothing that was worn by other slaves at Mount Vernon, a scene reenacted above by three interpreters. Enslaved men on Washington's farms received two shirts and two pairs of breeches each year. Slave women got two linen shifts and two skirts. Both also received a woolen jacket and one pair each of stockings and shoes. These garments were expected to last 12 months, despite being worn every day for field labor. Some of the female house servants received nicer attire made from printed fabric.

Unlike Kitty and Isaac, most married slaves at Mount Vernon did not live in the same household as their spouse. Some were married to people belonging to other plantations. Many had spouses living on one of Washington's other farms. Washington housed his slaves on the farm where they were assigned to work. For example, Sambo Anderson, who was also a carpenter, lived at the Mansion House Farm during the six-day workweek. His wife, Agnes, and their three children—Henky, Cecelia, and Anderson—lived about five miles away at River Farm, where they were all field laborers.

When the workday ended at sunset on Saturday, Sambo probably walked to River Farm to spend his time off with his wife and family. Other people traveled much farther to see their loved ones. On Sunday evening many of them walked through the night to return to work at dawn on Monday. Still others visited with friends or family, or hunted or fished or did other things on weekday nights. Washington did not mind how his slaves spent their time on Saturday nights, but he disapproved of their "night walking" on other evenings. Although he did not forbid it, he complained more than once that it left his slaves too tired to do their "duties of the day."

Most of the enslaved children at Mount Vernon lived with their mothers. Babies probably went to work with their mothers until they began to toddle around. Then they were left at home to be looked after by older siblings. Children did chores for their families—and sometimes for the overseers—such as fetching wood and water for cooking and washing. They also played with friends, but all that ended when they were between the ages of 11 and 14. Then they became part of a group called "working boys and girls." These young people helped adult laborers with such tasks as working on roads, cleaning bricks, baking bread, hauling manure, and making fences. After age 14, boys and girls were assigned adult duties. Skilled and household staff jobs often passed from father to son or mother to daughter. For example, when Doll, the enslaved cook who came to Mount Vernon with Martha Washington in 1759, became too old to work, her daughter Lucy took over the kitchen.

During visits with family and friends, the enslaved individuals at Mount Vernon must have enjoyed relaxing together away from the watchful eyes of their owner and

George Washington ordered his estate managers and overseers to "be particularly attentive to my Negroes in their sickness." His account books show many payments over the years for medical care for his slaves. Below, historical interpreters portray a sick man being treated by Dr. James Craik, who was also Washington's personal physician.

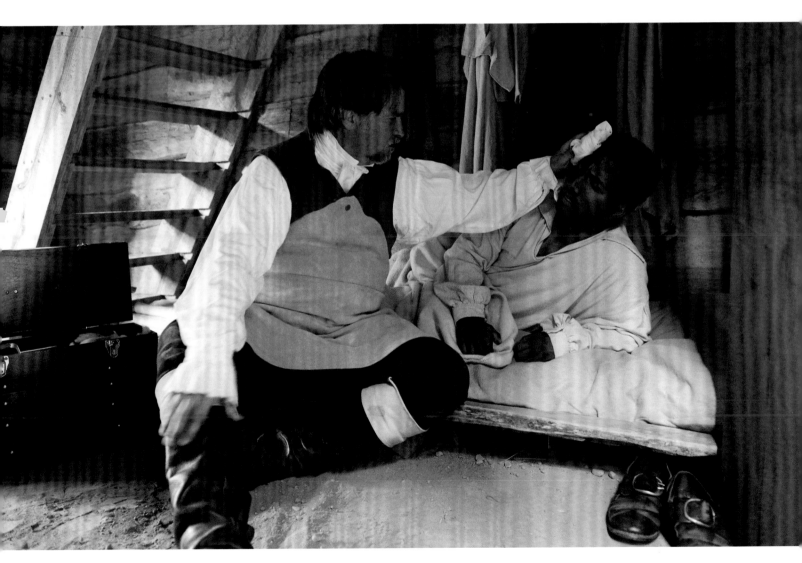

Two young interpreters play with clay marbles while another hops over their game at a log cabin built to replicate the field hands' quarters on Washington's outlying farms. Although this cabin looks sturdy enough, some of the actual slave cabins were so flimsy that when Washington wanted them moved to a different place, he told his manager the slaves could probably just pick them up and carry them.

his overseers. Excavated artifacts such as a jaw harp (a small musical instrument also known as a Jew's harp) and clay pipe fragments indicate that people played music and smoked tobacco in their free time. Children, and perhaps adults too, played games with clay marbles, which were also excavated from the site of a Mount Vernon slave quarter. A favorite outdoor game was "prisoner's base," a type of tag played by children and grownups.

A few of Washington's slaves may have used their personal time to learn how to read or to teach others to do so. The black overseers on his outlying farms, for example, were probably expected to read and write so they could prepare their weekly reports. Some of the house servants were probably literate as well. And at least one of Washington's field laborers could read. His name was Caesar, and he ran away from Mount Vernon several times in the 1790s. In 1796 Washington wrote from Philadelphia: "I see by the last week's report that Caesar has been absent six days. Is he a runaway? If so, it is probable he will escape altogether, as he can read, if not write." Yet Caesar did not escape forever. In 1798, Washington paid $25 to an unnamed person "for taking up Caesar, a runaway Negro," and returning him to Mount Vernon.

Caesar seems to have been a spiritual leader for the local black community, according to an advertisement posted while he was a runaway that described him as a preacher. George and Martha Washington apparently took no interest in their slaves' spiritual lives, but a French visitor noted that Mount Vernon slaves had contact with Christian groups including Methodists, Baptists, and Quakers. Slaves born in Africa may have brought Islamic or traditional African religious practices with them.

Singing and storytelling were popular pastimes in slave quarters. Martha Washington's grandson, who lived at Mount Vernon as a child, recalled hearing an elderly man named Jack "tell of days long past, of Afric's clime, and of Afric's wars, in which he . . . was made captive." Sambo Anderson was also African born. He was described as being "a bright mahogany color, with high cheekbones, and . . . stoutly made. His face was tattooed, and he wore in his ears rings which . . . were made of real Guinea gold." He probably came from West Africa, where Sambo is still a common man's name today. Sambo claimed he was "the son of a king." He told stories of how he was captured as a boy and brought to America on a slave ship. For Sambo and other enslaved Africans and African Americans, storytelling was more than just an entertaining way to pass the time. It also helped build pride, teach family histories, and pass on cultural values from one generation to the next.

Besides socializing and having fun, enslaved people at Mount Vernon used their limited leisure time for personal chores, such as cooking their meals, washing and mending their clothes, and tending to their own garden plots. Washington allotted his slaves a small patch of land near their quarters, and they used it to grow fruits and vegetables and raise chickens. He also allowed a few of his slaves to keep guns and hunt for wild birds and small game such as squirrels and rabbits. Some slaves fished in their spare time. The fresh produce, eggs, game, and fish would have been welcome additions to the slaves' basic diet of cornmeal and dried fish.

Costumed interpreters mix boiling water and grain, the first step in making whiskey. In 1797 George Washington had a whiskey distillery built next to his gristmill. Although Washington hired white men to manage the operation, most of the tasks were performed by a crew of enslaved African Americans. Hanson, Peter, Nat, Daniel, Timothy, and James were listed as laborers in the distillery. Ben and Forrester worked at the gristmill, where water-powered machinery ground wheat into flour and corn into meal.

Some Mount Vernon workers sold the food they raised or caught to their master for his table. Isaac, for example, sold dozens of chickens and gallons of honey to the Washingtons over the years. One fall Washington bought 132 birds from Sambo Anderson and Tom Davis, an enslaved bricklayer who hunted ducks on the Potomac River with his "great Newfoundland dog" named Gunner.

On Sunday mornings, Washington's slaves sometimes traveled nine miles to the port town of Alexandria to sell their chickens, eggs, and garden products. Some might also have sold items they made in their free time, such as brooms. Slaves from the surrounding countryside were permitted to peddle their goods at the market until nine o'clock in the morning, as long as they had a special pass from their master. With the money they earned, slaves could buy luxuries such as tea, sugar, teapots, cups, combs, or articles of clothing from shops in Alexandria. Washington's slaves also used their money to buy such things as fine flour, pork, and whiskey from him.

House servants and stable hands probably received cash tips from grateful guests at Mount Vernon. Sometimes Washington gave slaves gifts of money on Christmas day. He also paid his slaves when they had to work in their "off-duty" hours. One spring, for example, Washington recorded a payment to "seine haulers, fish carri-

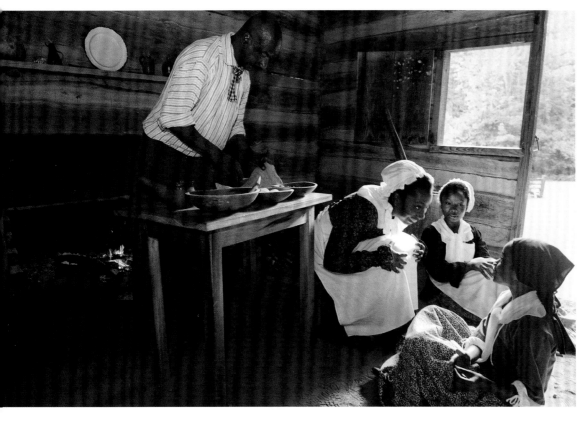

In an interpretation of slave family life, a mother tells a story to her daughters, while the father prepares a meal. Each adult slave at Mount Vernon received a daily food ration of about four cups of cornmeal and five to eight ounces of salted, dried herring. Those too young or too old to work were given half that amount. "It is not my wish or desire that my Negroes should have an ounce of meal more, nor less, than is sufficient to feed them plentifully," Washington stated.

ers," and "cleaners of fish" for working on four "Sundays and the Easter Holyday."

On at least one occasion, Mount Vernon slaves sold their teeth to make money. In 1784, Washington—whose own teeth were notoriously bad—paid several "Negroes" 122 shillings for nine teeth. He may have had these teeth transplanted into his own jaw to improve his appearance. Some of the teeth in Washington's dentures probably also came from the mouths of his own slaves. Today this seems horrifying, but in 18th-century America it was not unusual for wealthy people to buy teeth from the poor. In Europe the custom dated to the Middle Ages. Even so, the fact that some of Washington's laborers were willing to have their teeth yanked out of their heads to earn a few shillings reveals how desperate they were to improve their standard of living. No matter how hard they worked, they received barely enough to survive. They had no rights, and the few privileges they enjoyed could be taken away by their master at any time. Even in their "free" time, enslaved people were never truly free. Perhaps the worst thing of all would have been knowing that their children faced the same future.

HERCULES

HERCULES WAS George Washington's top chef. He learned to cook in Mount Vernon's kitchen. He was so good at it that when the President needed a chief cook for his "new habitation" in Philadelphia in 1790—at that time the capital of the United States—he had Hercules brought up from Virginia. Washington thought his enslaved cook much more presentable than the hired white ones he was employing at the time. Their "dirty figures," he worried, would not be "a pleasant sight" from the "entertaining rooms."

By contrast, Hercules "gloried in the cleanliness and nicety of his kitchen" and ruled it with "iron discipline." His culinary skills, along with his "good character and pleasing manners," won him the esteem of everyone in the Washington household. Hercules persuaded his master to let his teenage son, Richmond, come to Philadelphia as his assistant, even though Washington had a poor opinion of the boy. Hercules was also allowed to sell scraps—such as chicken feathers and bones or used tea leaves—from the presidential kitchen. He spent the money he earned on such luxuries as black silk waistcoats and a gold-headed cane.

Hercules relished his fame as the President's cook and walked proudly down the streets of Philadelphia in his finery. He made friends in the local black community, many of whom were free. Hercules hungered for freedom, too. Fancy clothes or not, he was still a slave. But he didn't intend to remain one.

Shortly before Washington stepped down as President, Hercules suddenly vanished. He was reported to have "absconded" in the early morning of February 22, 1797—his master's sixty-fifth birthday. Washington described the "running off of my cook" as a "most inconvenient thing to this family." He spent several years trying to track down Hercules and bring him back to Mount Vernon. But the prized chef was never heard from again.

Hercules left a young daughter at home at Mount Vernon. About six weeks after he ran away, a French visitor asked the girl if she was sad because she would never see her father again. Her answer surprised him: "Oh! Sir, I am very glad, because he is free now."

The elegantly dressed man in this painting is presumed to be Hercules, George Washington's enslaved cook. This picture is said to be the work of artist Gilbert Stuart, who also painted many portraits of Washington.

"TELL MUCLUS, AS FROM ME, THAT IF HIS **PRIDE** IS NOT A SUFFICIENT STIMULUS TO EXCITE HIM TO **INDUSTRY**, AND ADMONITION HAS NO EFFECT UPON HIM, THAT I HAVE DIRECTED YOU TO HAVE HIM **SEVERELY** PUNISHED."

Letter of George Washington to Anthony Whitting, 19 May 1793

CHAPTER 4

RESISTANCE AND CONTROL.

GEORGE WASHINGTON called his enslaved workers his "people" or his "family," but they were unique human beings, each with his or her own values and hopes and dreams. They yearned to live their lives as free men and women. Many of them ran away to be free.

A man named Boson was one of the first slaves mentioned as a runaway in Washington's records. In 1760 he twice went missing and was twice recaptured. The next year Peros, Cupid, Jack, and Neptune slipped away. Washington placed a newspaper advertisement offering a 40 shilling reward for their capture. In it he carefully described each man. Peros, he said, was 35 to 40 years old, with a "yellowish complexion . . . a very full round face, and full black beard." Cupid, about 23, was full faced and his skin was "inclined to be pimply." The other two men bore ethnic markings. Jack, about age 30, had a "small face, with cuts down each cheek, being his country marks." Neptune, age 25 or 30, was "thin jawed, his teeth straggling and filed sharp," and his back had "many small marks or dots running from both shoulders down to his waistband."

Cupid and Neptune talked in "very broken and unintelligible English," Washington wrote in the advertisement. He had bought them "from an African ship" only two years earlier. Jack, he noted, was also from Africa but he spoke "pretty good English, having been several years in the country." Peros spoke "much better" than the other three and was "esteemed a sensible, judicious Negro." The advertisement reported the size of each

George Washington had high expectations for himself and for everyone who worked for him. He insisted that "every laborer (male or female) does as much in the 24 hours as their strength, without endangering the health, or constitution, will allow of." To be at work "as soon as it is light," field hands had to get out of bed before sunup and tramp through darkness to their job site. They were expected to keep working—except for two meal breaks—until it was too dark to see.

runaway, and the clothes he was wearing when last seen. The men had left together on a Sunday, their day off from work. They knew they wouldn't be missed until that night or even the next morning if they were lucky.

The detailed descriptions in the advertisement show that Washington knew his slaves as distinct individuals. He was very familiar with Cupid, because Cupid had been gravely ill the year before he ran away. Washington arranged special care for him and personally checked on his condition. In one diary entry he wrote that he feared Cupid was "within a few hours of breathing his last." If Cupid felt grateful for his master's concern, however, it didn't stop him from escaping when he saw the chance. He and the other three men, Washington wrote in an injured tone, "went off without the least suspicion, provocation, or difference with anybody, or the least angry word or abuse from their overseers."

Between 1759 and 1799, at least 47 enslaved men and women ran away from Mount Vernon. A large group left in 1781, while George Washington was away fighting the Revolutionary War. That spring a British warship dropped anchor in the Potomac near the estate, and the captain promised freedom to any slaves who wished to leave. Three women and fourteen men—among them Sambo Anderson—sailed away with him. Many more of the Washingtons' slaves would probably have fled to freedom over the years had they not felt bound to Mount Vernon by strong family ties.

George Washington spared no expense in tracking down runaway slaves. He hated to lose valuable property. Many of the men and women who ran away from the Washingtons—including Cupid and his companions and Sambo Anderson—were eventually recaptured and returned to their owner. Some escaped for good. The most successful runaways tended to be those who could read and write or had a special skill, such as sewing or cooking, that they could support themselves with in the outside world.

Runaways brought back to Mount Vernon seem not to have faced harsh punishment, unless they were repeat offenders like Tom. Nonetheless, Washington saw it as an act of betrayal and ingratitude when his slaves ran away. He expected them to be loyal and deliver the same high performance he demanded from soldiers in the army. But in the army, Washington and his men fought for the greater good. His slaves, on the other hand, toiled for the exclusive good of George Washington. It was obvious to them that no matter how hard they worked, no matter how "diligent" they were, their lives would not change. They would remain slaves. But they did not accept their enslavement meekly.

Mount Vernon's slaves resisted slavery in a variety of ways besides running away. They were careless with tools, for example. After all, if your ax blade was dull or broken or lost you couldn't chop wood with it. They worked slowly, or not at all if they thought they could get away with it. They also helped themselves to their master's fruit and grain, his pigs and lambs, his linen and wool.

It frustrated Washington that his slaves did not share his work ethic and his desire

for order and perfection. "Nothing pleases me better than to see [my farms] in good order and everything trim, handsome, and thriving about them," he lectured one of his managers. "Nor nothing hurts me more than to find them otherwise and the tools and implements laying wherever they were last used, exposed to injuries from rain, sun, etc." He reminded another to "keep everyone in their places and to their duty." Otherwise, he warned, the slaves would push the limits to "see how far they durst [dare] go."

Most of all Washington deplored the "spirit of thieving and housebreaking . . . among my people." He believed he fed, clothed, and housed his "people" as well as or better than any other slave owner in the region. As far as he was concerned, they were entitled to nothing more. From the slaves' point of view, however, what they were given by their master was totally inadequate. So they took it upon themselves to make up the difference. Meat disappeared from the meat house and corn vanished from the corn loft, as did cherries from the orchards and nails from construction sites. "I cannot conceive how it is possible that 6000 twelve penny nails could be used in the corn house at River Plantation," Washington fumed. To him these were acts of theft, pure and simple. Mount Vernon's enslaved people no doubt saw the matter differently. They felt they had earned a share of the goods their labor had produced.

Washington suspected that many stolen items—at least those that weren't eaten right away—were sold or traded by slaves to "underling shop keepers" in nearby

It took a lot of courage for slaves to run away from their masters, a scene re-created here by historical interpreters. Some slaves journeyed hundreds of miles away, knowing they might never see their families again. Others stayed closer to home and hid in the woods. Many of the slaves who fled from Mount Vernon were recaptured and returned to the Washingtons. Some, however, escaped for good.

In their spare time, enslaved workers at Mount Vernon might have caught fresh fish using a net like this one. George Washington also operated a commercial fishing business along Mount Vernon's shoreline. For about six weeks in the spring the Potomac River teemed with herring and shad, and almost everyone on the plantation pitched in to haul in and preserve the catch. Using large, heavy fishing nets called seines, Washington's workers netted 1.3 million herring in 1772. Washington set aside part of the catch to supply food for his enslaved laborers in the coming year, and he sold the rest. For many years, the fishery was Washington's most profitable business.

Alexandria. He upbraided his overseers for "frolicking at the expense of my business" when they should have been "watching the barns, visiting the Negro quarters at unexpected hours [or] waylaying the roads."

Washington could have put a stop to most of the slacking off and stealing if he had been willing to punish his slaves more severely. Before the Revolutionary War he didn't

hesitate to ship off and sell unruly slaves like Tom or to allow his overseers to flog slaves for misbehavior. In 1758, for example, the overseer in charge of Washington's enslaved carpenters assured his employer that "I have minded 'em all I possibly could and has whipt 'em when I could see a fault." Washington had grown up seeing these brutal punishments used to scare slaves into obedience. Like other slaveholders of his time and place, he considered them standard practice.

During the fight for American independence, however, Washington's ideas on how blacks should be treated began to change. He resolved never again to sell slaves against their will. He also ordered his overseers to put away their whips. In the future the lash was to be used only as a last resort and only with his written permission. It was easier to prevent "all irregularities and improper conduct," Washington told one estate manager, "by watchfulness and admonition than by severity and certainly must be more agreeable to every feeling mind in the practice of them."

A white man raises his arm to beat a black man's bare back in this painting from the early 1800s. George Washington eventually forbade Mount Vernon overseers from whipping slaves, except as a last resort.

Unfortunately Washington's overseers did not always obey his rule against flogging, especially during his long absences from Mount Vernon. And Washington himself continued to issue threats of harsh punishment from time to time. In 1793, for instance, he told his manager to tell a bricklayer named Muclus "that if his pride is not a sufficient stimulus to excite him to industry, and admonition has no effect upon him, that I have directed you to have him severely punished and placed under one of the overseers as a common hoe Negro." It was understood that by "severely punished" Washington meant a whipping, a term he avoided putting to paper. That same year he gave instructions on how to deal with an enslaved teenager named Ben who was suspected of theft: "He, his father and mother (who I dare say are his receivers) may be told in explicit language that if a stop is not put to his rogueries, and other villainies by fair means and shortly, that I will ship him off . . . for the West Indies, where he will have no opportunity of playing such pranks as he is at present engaged in."

Ben was still at Mount Vernon, working as a ditch digger, in the summer of 1799. So we know Washington did not make good on this threat.

Once they no longer lived in constant fear of frequent beatings or of being sold away from family and friends, Mount Vernon's slaves had even less reason to cooperate. "Watchfulness and admonition" were not enough to motivate people to work hard when they had no economic incentive to do so. Yet despite their resistance to their master's planning and prodding, Washington's enslaved laborers accomplished a huge amount of work over the years. Under his direction, they became some of the most talented farmers, gardeners, fishermen, builders, and animal breeders in Virginia and beyond. Their labor helped make him rich. That in turn helped him become a leader, first in Virginia and then in the United States. But there was nothing in it for the slaves.

CHARLOTTE

CHARLOTTE, an enslaved seamstress at Mount Vernon, wasn't afraid to speak up for herself. One spring day she was in Alexandria, probably on an errand for the Washingtons, when a white woman named Mrs. MacIver recognized the red-and-white dress she was wearing. It was the same dress that had been stolen from Mrs. MacIver two years earlier. Charlotte had bought it from another slave and had nothing to do with the theft. But when Mrs. MacIver insisted on taking a closer look at the garment, Charlotte refused to let her. Not only that, Charlotte threatened to "flog" the other woman and called her "abusive and contemptuous" names, according to a letter Mrs. MacIver's husband wrote to George Washington about the matter.

Apparently Charlotte was not punished for her clash with Mrs. MacIver. But a few years later, when Washington was President, Charlotte's fiery spirit did land her in trouble. In his weekly report, farm manager Anthony Whitting wrote Washington that he had given Charlotte "a very good whipping" with a hickory switch after they had a disagreement and she became "very impudent." He beat her again two days later when she

refused to do some sewing. Outraged by the beating, Charlotte threatened him "with informing Lady Washington when she comes home and says she has not been whipped for 14 years." Nonetheless, Whitting said, he was "determined to lower her spirit or skin her back."

Washington's reply shows just how vulnerable slaves were to abuse by their overseers. "Your treatment of Charlotte was very proper," Washington wrote to Whitting, adding that "if she, or any other of the servants will not do their duty by fair means, or are impertinent, correction . . . must be administered." It is a chilling response, especially considering that Washington later described Whitting as someone who "drank freely [and] kept bad company."

Despite her quick temper, Charlotte must have been one of Mount Vernon's most trusted servants. Six years after the incident with Whitting, she was one of four slaves who attended George Washington as he lay on his deathbed.

When Charlotte and the other seamstresses made fewer shirts than usual, Washington warned he would send them to the outlying farms to "be placed as common laborers under the overseers' threat"—a scene depicted in this 1798 sketch.

"IT HAS BEEN REPRESENTED TO ME THAT THE **FREE** NEGROES WHO HAVE SERVED IN THIS ARMY, ARE VERY MUCH **DISSATISFIED** AT BEING **DISCARDED."**

Letter of George Washington to
John Hancock, 31 December 1775

CHAPTER 5

A CHANGE OF HEART

WHEN HE LEFT MOUNT VERNON to lead the fight for American independence, George Washington still accepted slavery as a matter of course. So he was surely astonished by what he saw when he and his enslaved servant William Lee arrived at army headquarters in Cambridge, Massachusetts, in July 1775. Awaiting his command were not only white troops but black ones as well, toting guns and ready for action. To the 43-year-old plantation master, who had been raised to think of African Americans as inferior, the sight of so many dark-skinned men bearing arms must have been jarring.

The first shots of the Revolutionary War had been fired three months earlier in the Massachusetts towns of Lexington and Concord. Since then, white and black men alike had rallied to the patriot cause and joined New England militias. In the first months of his command, Washington banned black militiamen from the new Continental Army he was organizing. In November 1775 he issued an order that "neither Negroes, boys unable to bear arms, nor old men unfit to endure the fatigues of the campaign, are to be enlisted." But the very next month he gave a new order allowing free black men to enlist after all. In a letter to John Hancock, the president of the Continental Congress, Washington explained why. "It has been represented to me," he wrote, "that the free Negroes who have served in this army are very much dissatisfied at being discarded." He added

The sight of armed black soldiers must have startled George Washington when he arrived in Massachusetts in July 1775 to take charge of the new Continental Army. During the Revolutionary War, about 5,000 black troops served in the Continental Army. As many as 15,000 enslaved men, women, and children may have run away from their owners to join the British forces, who promised them freedom.

During the Revolutionary War, Martha Washington joined her husband every year at his army's winter camp, including the bitter winter at Valley Forge, Pennsylvania, depicted above. Fighting was at a standstill during these months. Martha always brought several slaves from Mount Vernon with her to help cook and clean and serve Washington's officers and other guests at social functions.

that he feared the blacks might join the British army if the Americans did not take them.

Washington's about-face suggests that it didn't take very long for him to see African Americans in a new light once he was away from Virginia. He recognized the black soldiers' ability, and he knew his army would need every capable soldier it could get—regardless of race—to beat the British. Washington's decision opened the way for about 5,000 black troops to serve in the Continental Army during the Revolutionary War. During the long conflict, blacks fought and died alongside whites in the name of freedom. "You never see a regiment in which there are not Negroes," noted a foreign officer.

Around the time he decided to admit black soldiers into the army, another thing happened that hints at how quickly Washington's ideas about African Americans were evolving. He received a poem in the mail. It was a glowing tribute to him penned by an African-born slave and poet named Phillis Wheatley, who lived in nearby Boston. Washington sent her a letter of thanks, in which he praised her "elegant lines" and "genius." At the end of it he wrote: "If you should ever come to Cambridge, or near Head Quarters, I shall be happy to see a person so favored by the Muses . . . I am, with great respect, your obedient humble servant, G. Washington." What makes Washington's response so remarkable is that he addressed Wheatley in terms of social equality. Even more extraordinary was his invitation to pay him a visit. It appears she did so a few months later and was given a "very courteous reception." Such a thing would have been unimaginable in Virginia.

The Revolutionary War kept George Washington away from Mount Vernon for more than eight years. During this time, his feelings about slavery changed a great deal. He went from being an unthinking slaveholder to a very uneasy one. By the end of 1775 he could no longer stomach breaking up slave families. When he agreed to accept a slave in payment for a debt and then learned that the slave was "so attached to his wife and children that he had repeatedly declared he had rather die than leave them," he promised to buy the whole family—which he did not need—rather than separate them. A few years later Washington confessed to his cousin Lund that he longed "every day . . . more and more to get clear of" owning slaves. Another time the two men exchanged letters about the possibility of selling slaves to raise cash, but then Washington decided he would not sell them "without their consent."

A portrait of Phillis Wheatley appears opposite the title page in this collection of her poems published in 1773. Born in Africa, shipped to America, and sold into slavery as a child, Wheatley was the first African American to publish a book of poems. During the Revolution she sent General George Washington a poem that deeply impressed him.

Over the course of the Revolution, Washington probably had many experiences—including his contact with Phillis Wheatley—that broadened his thinking about the cruel system of labor he had accepted without question his whole life. For one thing, he spent much of the war in the North, where slavery was much less common than in the South. There he saw successful farming operations that did not rely on enslaved laborers. Washington was also influenced by the idealism of some of his young officers, including the Marquis de Lafayette, who passionately opposed slavery. The courage, intelligence, and patriotism of the black soldiers under his command must also have made a deep impression on him. Almost certainly Washington recognized the irony of his position: He was leading the struggle for the revolutionary ideals of "life, liberty, and the pursuit of happiness," while he himself continued to hold fellow human beings in bondage.

Even as he longed "to get clear of" slave ownership, however, Washington kept William Lee at his side throughout the war. And when Martha Washington joined her husband every year at his winter camp, she always took several of Mount Vernon's household slaves with her. As they waited on General Washington and his officers, the enslaved African Americans likely heard impassioned discussions about the right to live free from British tyranny. To their ears such words must have sounded hollow. They also craved freedom. It was clear, however, that the basic human rights deemed worth dying for by Washington and the other Founding Fathers would not be extended to them.

America won its independence in October 1781, when the British army surrendered in Yorktown, Virginia. Washington retired from the military two years later, after a peace treaty was signed. On Christmas Eve 1783, he and William Lee finally returned home. Over the next five years, Washington devoted most of his time to improving Mount Vernon's buildings and fields, and to experimenting with new crops. He truly loved being a farmer. But he was more troubled than ever by slavery. On the one hand, he depended on slave labor to support his wealthy lifestyle. He still viewed his slaves as valuable property. He still expected them to work hard and produce much in exchange for the food, clothing, and shelter he provided. On the other hand, he was increasingly aware that slavery was unjust.

Washington was reminded of this injustice by the abolitionists who approached him after the war. Abolitionists believed that slavery was evil and should be ended. Over the years, several of them tried to enlist Washington, now a national hero, in their cause. He assured them privately that "there is not a man living who wishes more sincerely than I do" to see slavery eliminated. He expressed his intention never "to possess another slave

After the Revolutionary War, Washington's French ally the Marquis de Lafayette visited him at Mount Vernon, a scene portrayed here. Ardently opposed to slavery, Lafayette later declared "I would never have drawn my sword in the cause of America, if I could have conceived that thereby I was founding a land of slavery."

by purchase." He hoped the Virginia legislature would set up a plan to abolish slavery by "slow, sure, and imperceptible degrees." But Washington could never bring himself to take a public stand in favor of freeing, or emancipating, slaves. For one thing, he had his reputation to protect. He wasn't ready to free his own slaves, and he knew if he spoke out publicly in favor of emancipation while still being a slave owner, he would be called a hypocrite—a person who pretends to be honorable but is not.

The main reason Washington kept quiet about slavery, however, was because he thought the issue had the power to tear apart the fragile young nation he had worked so hard to build. At the beginning of the Revolutionary War, slavery was legal in all thirteen colonies. Then in 1776 Vermont abolished it outright. Over the next decade, most of the other northern states gradually emancipated slaves. Georgia and other southern states, however, were determined to preserve "this species of property." Washington's first priority was keeping his beloved country together. So even though he supported emancipation in theory, he thought it best for the nation if he remained silent on the matter. He told a friend, "I shall frankly declare to you that I do not like even to think, much less talk of it."

On April 14, 1789, George Washington received word that he had been elected the first President of the United States. Two days later he left Mount Vernon and headed to New York City, which was then the nation's capital. Martha Washington followed a few weeks after, accompanied by six slaves, including her 16-year-old maid, Oney Judge, and Oney's older brother Austin, a waiter. When they departed, Martha's nephew wrote, "the servants of the house and a number of field Negroes made their appearance to take leave of their mistress—numbers of these wretches were most affected, and my aunt equally so." It's no wonder that some slaves were so upset. They were saying goodbye to family members who were going far away for a long time. Oney and Austin's mother, Betty, must have been among those with a heavy heart that day.

When the nation's capital was transferred to Philadelphia in 1790, the Washingtons took along most of the slaves who had served them in New York. They also had their cook Hercules brought up from Mount Vernon to be top chef at the new presidential mansion.

The move to Philadelphia put Washington in an awkward legal situation. Pennsylvania law declared that adult slaves could claim their freedom after living in

In Philadelphia, George Washington's enslaved African-American servants roamed freely through the city as they ran errands for their master and mistress. Washington even gave Hercules, Austin, and Oney Judge money to attend the theater by themselves. Such experiences may well have strengthened their desire for freedom.

the state for six months. Washington wanted to hang onto his "property." He wrote his secretary Tobias Lear that he did not think his slaves "would be benefited by the change, yet the idea of freedom might be too great a temptation for them to resist." So he decided to invent excuses to send the slaves back to Virginia from time to time, to prevent them from achieving the six-month residency. "I wish to have it accomplished under pretext that may deceive both them [the slaves] and the public," he instructed Lear, adding that he wanted the plan "known to none but yourself and Mrs. Washington." His desire for secrecy is not surprising—he knew it would tarnish his reputation if the public learned the President of the United States was spiriting his slaves away to dodge the law.

It is a sign of Washington's conflicted attitude toward slavery that even as he schemed to keep some of his slaves from being freed by Pennsylvania law, he considered several ways to emancipate Mount Vernon's field hands. In 1793, for example, he proposed renting the plantation's four outlying farms to tenant farmers. His idea was to then free his slaves, who in turn would be hired by the tenants to work the land. That way the freed slaves could support themselves. Washington wrote to a number of potential tenants about the plan, but nothing came of it. Mount Vernon's "people" remained enslaved.

WILLIAM LEE

IF GEORGE WASHINGTON was really the "best horseman of his age," as Thomas Jefferson once said, then William Lee must have been a close second. Otherwise he never could have kept up with his master. From the time Washington purchased him in 1768 until after the Revolutionary War, William Lee was never far from his owner's side, whether on horseback or on foot. Over the years he became Washington's most trusted slave.

Also called Will or Billy, Lee served as Washington's personal servant. He laid out his master's clothes every morning, brushed his hair, and tied it back with a ribbon. After breakfast he rode with Washington on his daily inspection of Mount Vernon's farms. Lee traveled with his master on rugged expeditions to the wilderness and on business trips to Williamsburg. During foxhunting season, he was Washington's huntsman. His job was to manage the pack of hounds pursuing the fox, and he followed them at breakneck speed through thickets and woods.

When George Washington galloped off to the Revolutionary War, Billy Lee went with him, of course. Lee remained the general's constant companion throughout the long struggle, sharing the hardships of Valley Forge and the triumph at Yorktown. During the war, Lee fell in love with a free black woman named Margaret Thomas, a seamstress and washerwoman. After he returned to Mount Vernon, he asked his master to allow her to join him there. Washington didn't like the woman, but he could not "refuse [Lee's] request . . . as he has lived with me so long and followed my fortunes through the war with fidelity." He arranged for Margaret's passage to Virginia, but no evidence exists that she actually came.

In 1785 Lee slipped and broke his knee while he was out surveying land with Washington. Three years later he fell again and broke his other knee, which left him crippled. Lee made the trip to New York after Washington was elected President, but his injuries limited his usefulness to his master. He was eventually sent back to Mount Vernon, where he spent his remaining years making and repairing shoes for the other enslaved people on the estate.

In this engraving from about 1785, General George Washington stands outside a military camp tent with the Declaration of Independence in his hand. The black man with the horse may represent Washington's slave William Lee, his steady companion throughout the Revolutionary War.

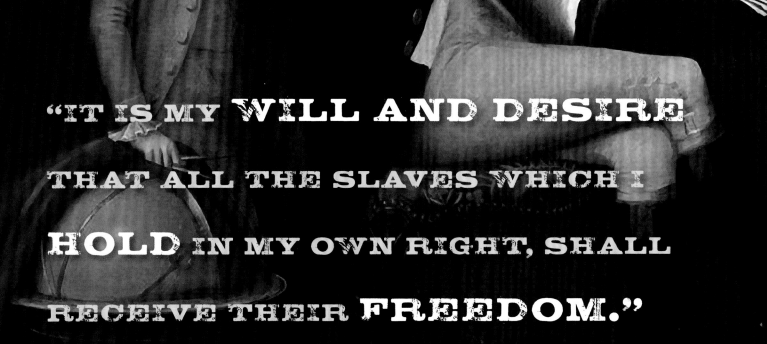

"IT IS MY **WILL AND DESIRE** THAT ALL THE SLAVES WHICH I **HOLD** IN MY OWN RIGHT, SHALL RECEIVE THEIR **FREEDOM.**"

George Washington's Last Will and Testament, 9 July 1799

CHAPTER 6

LIBERTY AT LAST

George Washington, shown here with his wife's grandson, George Washington Parke Custis (Washy), was increasingly troubled by slavery in his later years. Meanwhile his slaves dreamed of freedom. In 1797 some confided to a visiting Frenchman that "they hoped they would no longer be slaves in ten years."

AFTER SERVING TWO TERMS as President, George Washington looked forward to leaving political life behind and spending the rest of his days as a gentleman farmer at Mount Vernon. In March 1797 he and Martha and their grandchildren and slaves piled into coaches and set off for Virginia. Oney Judge was not with them. As Washington had feared, freedom had proved "too great a temptation" for her in Philadelphia. The previous year she had slipped away from the presidential mansion and escaped.

Oney eventually made her way to New Hampshire, where she used her skills as a seamstress to support herself. Washington went to great lengths to have the young woman recaptured, but she never returned to Mount Vernon. Both he and Martha felt betrayed by Oney's disappearance. Washington complained of "the ingratitude of the girl, who was brought up and treated more like a child than a servant." He seemed not to understand that no matter how well he treated his slaves, they naturally longed to be free.

Despite his blind spot when it came to his own slaves, by the last decade of his life Washington seems to have sincerely believed that slavery was morally wrong. He confided to a close friend, "The unfortunate condition of the persons, whose labor in part I employed, has been the only unavoidable subject of regret." He went on to mention his concern about the "justice of the Creator," which suggests that he found slavery at odds with his religious beliefs. Another time he wrote that he "earnestly" wished to "liberate a certain species of

Founding Fathers Thomas Jefferson (top), George Mason (middle), and James Madison (bottom) all claimed to hate slavery. They all remained slave owners, however, and they passed down slaves to their heirs.

property which I possess, very repugnantly to my own feelings."

On the practical side, Washington viewed slavery as a bad economic deal. Over the years, Mount Vernon's slave population had soared as more children were born. By 1799, the plantation was home to more than 300 slaves. Of these, nearly half were too old or too young to work. Washington calculated that he paid more to feed and clothe Mount Vernon's enslaved community than he gained in profit from their labor. "It is demonstratively clear," he fretted, "that on this estate . . . I have more working Negroes by a full moiety [half], than can be employed to any advantage in the farming system . . . To sell the overplus I cannot, because I am principled against this kind of traffic in the human species. To hire them out, is almost as bad, because they could not be disposed of in families to any advantage, and to disperse [break up] the families I have an aversion. What then is to be done? Something must, or I shall be ruined."

Besides his moral and economic misgivings, there was another reason that slavery gnawed at Washington's mind. He cared deeply about honor, and he was anxious "that no reproach may attach itself to me when I have taken my departure for the land of spirits." He worried that his ownership of slaves would be a blight on his historical reputation.

Washington was not the only Founding Father who wrestled with the problem of slavery. Fellow Virginians George Mason, Thomas Jefferson, and James Madison were also slaveholders. Like Washington, these three Revolutionary leaders had a kind of split personality when it came to slavery. They knew that their ownership of fellow human beings clashed with their principles of freedom and equality. They all claimed to detest slavery. Mason described it as a "slow poison, which is daily contaminating the minds and morals of our people." Jefferson, the author of the Declaration of Independence, called slavery an "abominable crime." Madison pronounced it the "most oppressive dominion ever exercised by man over man." All three men favored the gradual emancipation of slaves. But none of them could see his way clear to actually freeing all of his slaves. Only one slave-owning Founding Father found the courage to do that.

In the summer of 1799, George Washington drew up a farm-by-farm list of all Mount Vernon's enslaved people. He jotted down each individual's name and age. If a slave was married, he noted the spouse's name. After Washington finished the list, he shut himself in his study and tackled the issue he had grappled with for some 25 years. He had come a long way from the boy who took slavery for granted, from the callous master who bought and sold slaves without a second thought. Now he had finally decided to reject slavery. He did so by drafting a new will. He worked on it for several days, and he wrote it alone, every word of all 29 pages with his own hand. He signed the bottom of almost every page—he missed one—to make sure his intent would not be questioned. In this document he announced, "It is my will and desire that all the slaves which I hold in my *own right*, shall receive their freedom."

Washington could not free all of Mount Vernon's slaves because he did not own them all. Of the 317 slaves on his list, only 123 belonged to him outright. Forty-one were rented and would have to be returned to their owners. The remaining 153 slaves belonged to the dower share of property Martha had received from the estate of her first husband, Daniel Parke Custis. By law, the dower slaves were Martha's only while she lived. After her death, they would revert to the Custis family estate and be divided among her four grandchildren.

Over the years, the Washington slaves and dower slaves had intermarried and had children. Isaac, for example, belonged to Washington. His wife, Kitty, was a dower slave. Because a slave's status came from his or her mother, Isaac and Kitty's nine daughters were also dower slaves, as were the daughters' children. Washington knew that Isaac's family and many others would be broken up when his own slaves were freed. That's because the dower slaves would remain in bondage unless the Custis heirs decided to free them, and that was highly unlikely. This may be one reason Washington waited as long as he did to emancipate his own slaves. He wanted to delay the "disagreeable consequences" of the coming separations for as long as possible. For this reason he also specified that the freeing of his slaves not take place until after Martha's death. He wanted to spare her from witnessing the slave families' "most painful sensations."

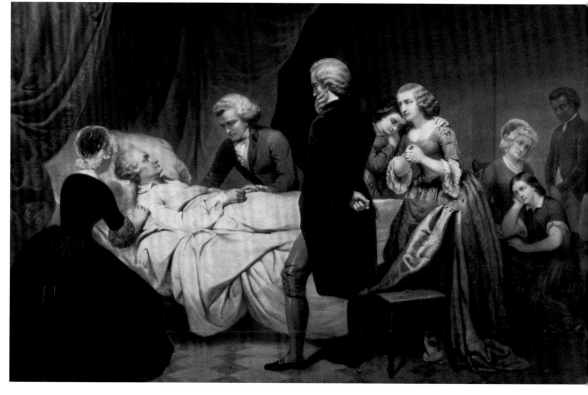

Created more than 50 years after Washington died, this deathbed scene shows him surrounded by friends and family. In reality the only people in the room with him were his wife; his doctor, James Craik; his secretary, Tobias Lear; and four enslaved servants: Caroline, Charlotte, Molly, and Christopher Sheels.

In the will, Washington stipulated that people too sick or old to work were to be "comfortably fed and clothed by my heirs while they live." He ordered that younger slaves, before being freed, should "be taught to read and write and to be brought up to some useful occupation." Washington may have suspected that his relatives and perhaps even his wife might try to ignore these instructions. (Martha appears not to have shared his disgust for slavery.) So he used strong language to make it crystal clear that he expected his directions to be honored: "I do moreover most pointedly, and most solemnly enjoin it upon my Executors . . . to see that this clause respecting slaves, and every part thereof be religiously fulfilled."

Washington singled out one slave in his will. He gave William Lee immediate freedom and left him thirty dollars per year "as a testimony of my sense of his attachment to me, and for his faithful services during the Revolutionary War."

Five months after writing his will, Washington rode out to inspect his farms on a snowy winter day and came home soaked and shivering. The following day he worked outdoors, even though it snowed again. That evening he was hoarse, and he woke during the night, struggling to breathe. At dawn Caroline, a housemaid, entered the Washingtons' bedroom to kindle a fire. Martha sent her to find Washington's secretary, Tobias Lear, who sent a slave to Alexandria to fetch James Craik, Washington's longtime doctor and friend. As the day wore on, Washington fought harder for every breath.

At one point that afternoon, Washington asked Martha to retrieve two wills from the desk in his study. He looked them over and then asked her to burn one. The will that remained was the one he had drawn up over the summer, which freed his slaves.

Washington died as he had lived, surrounded by enslaved people. Caroline, Charlotte, Molly, and Christopher Sheels attended him throughout the day. Christopher had replaced William Lee as Washington's valet. At one point Washington noticed that the young man looked tired—he had been standing by his master's bedside since morning—and motioned for him to sit down. Washington died around ten o'clock that evening. Christopher removed the keys from his master's pockets and handed them to Tobias Lear. It was December 14, 1799.

The next day, Christopher Sheels probably washed Washington's body and prepared it for burial. He, Frank Lee, and a 15-year-old named Marcus were issued new shoes, probably so that they would look respectable while they served guests at the funeral. The solemn ceremony was held at Mount Vernon four days after Washington's death. Two enslaved grooms, dressed in black, led Washington's horse in the funeral procession from the mansion to the family tomb. One was a 24-year-old named Cyrus. The other was Caroline's 15-year-old son, Wilson. Except for Frank Lee, all of the slaves mentioned in accounts of Washington's last day and funeral were dower slaves. None of them would be freed by Washington's will.

It is tempting to judge George Washington for not liberating his slaves during his lifetime, for continuing to hold human beings in bondage even after he knew it was wrong. By the standards of our own time, it can seem he did too little too late. But considering his time and place, Washington's decision to free his enslaved people was actually quite daring. Of all the slave-owning Founding Fathers, only he had the courage to listen to his conscience and turn his back on slavery. Only he dared to truly embrace the ideals of the American Revolution. Washington's will expressed his belief that Thomas Jefferson's famous words in the Declaration of Independence—"that all Men are created equal, that they are endowed by their Creator with certain unalienable Rights, that among these are Life, Liberty, and the Pursuit of Happiness"—applied to all men, regardless of race. He hoped it would set an example for his slave-holding family, neighbors, and peers. He knew it would serve as his final message to the country that he loved and to which he had dedicated his life.

The first page of George Washington's Last Will and Testament, in which he freed his slaves. He wrote every word of its 29 pages with his own hand.

CHRISTOPHER SHEELS

AFTER WILLIAM LEE became too disabled to fulfill his duties, George Washington knew it wouldn't be easy finding a suitable replacement for him. Washington wanted someone who could act as a butler as well as his valet. He was looking for "nothing short of excellent qualities and a man of good appearance." Eventually he selected Christopher Sheels for the job.

Christopher was a third-generation Mount Vernon slave. His mother, Alice, was a spinner. His grandmother, Doll, was the cook Martha Washington had brought with her to Mount Vernon as a bride. In spring 1789, after George Washington was sworn in as President, he had 14-year-old Christopher brought to New York to serve as a waiter in the presidential household. When the Washingtons moved to Philadelphia the next year, they took Christopher with them. In time he took over the position of personal servant to his master.

After Washington retired as President, Christopher Sheels was bitten by a sick dog at Mount Vernon. Washington was concerned the dog had rabies, and he regarded the young man highly enough to send him back to Pennsylvania to see a doctor "celebrated for curing persons bitten by mad animals." In a note to the doctor, Washington promised to "pay whatever is your charge" and explained that "besides the call of humanity, I am particularly anxious for his cure, he being my own body servant." A few months later Washington took "pleasure in informing" a friend that Christopher had "remained perfectly well ever since."

When Christopher asked permission to marry "a mulatto girl" on another plantation who was "well spoken of," Washington consented to the match. Apparently both Christopher and his bride could read and write. In September 1799 he received a note from her referring to their plans to flee together aboard a ship. Unfortunately, Christopher dropped the note in the yard. Washington found it and foiled their escape.

There is no evidence that Washington punished Christopher. Almost certainly he forgave him, for he kept the young man as his personal servant. And it was Christopher Sheels who kept the death watch by his master's bedside just three months later.

Dressed in livery, the African-American slave in this detail from a 1796 portrait of the Washington family may depict Christopher Sheels, or possibly William Lee.

EPILOGUE

NOT LONG AFTER GEORGE WASHINGTON'S death, his will was made public and his slaves learned that they would be freed as soon as Martha Washington died. Martha worried that some of the slaves might be tempted to hurry things along. She confided to Abigail Adams, wife of President John Adams, that "she did not feel as though her life was safe in their hands" since many of them "would be told that it was their interest to get rid of her." So Martha decided to go ahead and emancipate her husband's enslaved men, women, and children. In December of 1800, she signed the order that liberated them on January 1, 1801.

We know very little about what happened to these people after their emancipation. Some of them chose to stay at Mount Vernon. Frank and William Lee, for example, lived on the estate the rest of their lives. William died in 1810, Frank in 1821. As Washington directed in his will, funds from his estate were used to feed, clothe, and provide medical care for elderly and sickly slaves until the early 1830s.

Some of Washington's freed people settled near the estate, perhaps so they could remain close to relatives who were dower slaves. Sambo Anderson, whose wife and children were dower slaves, stayed in the Mount Vernon area. He made his living by hunting wild game, which he sold to hotels and "the most respectable families in Alexandria." In time he earned enough money to buy the freedom of two of his grandchildren and three of his great-grandchildren. At some point Letty, a field laborer from Muddy Hole Farm, moved to

Alexandria with her children Billy, Henry, and Nila. As a young man, Billy was described as having a mermaid tattoo, which suggests he might have found seafaring work. Suckey Bay's daughter Nancy, from River Farm, eventually married a free black man from Maryland named Charles Quander. Some of their descendants still live in the Mount Vernon area today.

Marcus, the teenage dower slave who was given new shoes for Washington's funeral, took his fate into his own hands and ran away from Mount Vernon in 1800. After Martha Washington died in May 1802, the rest of the dower slaves were divided among her four grandchildren. This separated some of them from their loved ones forever. Most of the dower slaves, including Charlotte the seamstress, Davy the overseer, and Christopher Sheels were never heard of again. Neither was Christopher's grandmother, Doll, or Frank Lee's wife, Lucy. We do know that Lucy and Frank's son Philip Lee served as a valet to Martha Washington's grandson, George Washington Parke Custis. Caroline and her daughter Rachel also ended up in Custis's household.

After Martha's death, George Washington's nephew Bushrod Washington inherited the Mansion House property. The rest of the Mount Vernon estate was divided among several other heirs. Over the years, the mansion and outbuildings fell into decay, until the Mount Vernon Ladies' Association took possession of the estate in 1860 and began the preservation and restoration work that still continues.

Today at Mount Vernon, a granite column ringed by a small boxwood garden marks the site of the burial ground used by George Washington's slaves. Although the graves are unmarked, it is believed that William Lee is among the people buried at the site. It is a quiet place, a good place to remember and honor the enslaved African Americans who once lived and worked on this riverside plantation. Their labor and sacrifices contributed to the building of our nation as surely as the leadership of their famous master.

This ambrotype of an African-American man named Tom was taken in the mid-19th century. Tom is believed to have been one of Martha Washington's dower slaves at Mount Vernon.

George Washington compiled this farm-by-farm list of Mount Vernon's slaves in the summer of 1799.

ENDNOTE

I AM CONTINUING A JOURNEY that began centuries ago. Recently I traced my family's DNA back to its maternal roots. There I found our band of ancestors safely nestled in the Sudan near today's Egyptian border. Some of them migrated north and east into today's Middle East and beyond through Asia and eventually into North America. Others undoubtedly migrated westward to the African coast, and some into the bondage of the slave trade.

One of my slave ancestors ended up in one of America's historic homes. Caroline Branham was a personal maid to Martha Washington.

What can I tell you of my Mount Vernon ancestor, my Caroline? I've been asked many times how I feel about sharing her story. Indeed, it is quite a story. My Caroline came from the home of Daniel Custis, part of a large family of Branham girls, all listed as mulattoes. She married Peter Hardiman, who was rented from Dr. David Stuart, of Washington City. When Washington planned to return Peter to Stuart, Peter stood his ground with Washington and told him he would remain at Mount Vernon, for he loved Caroline, wanted to marry her, and would not be persuaded to leave. Washington understood. Caroline and Peter were fancy in dress; they were accomplished in duties. They were the makers of beds and shirts and good manners before guests, and the keepers of horses and mules on nearby properties. They longed for the simplest things—privacy, freedom, and respect.

The specter of slavery scratches my heart. My ancestors, once walking on the Sahara Desert, would find it difficult to imagine the paths given to their descendants. Reflecting on it all, I find that I, like Caroline, long for something. We are all so connected. We all want to know that we are loved and of value. The institution of slavery has united our nation in relationships that bind us as brothers and sisters under the skin. We all deserve to have a place at the table; one that makes no distinction between black and white, between memories of the enslaved or those who forced their labor. I long for truth, and I long for the pure song of joy that comes with its discovery. I long for an end to longing and the beginning of knowing that where one stops the other begins. I embrace my connection with my Caroline, across generations, and I embrace her story, for the truth and love that comes from its telling.

ZSun-nee Matema is a world history instructor in Baltimore, Maryland, and founding director of AFRIAsia: The Intercultural Education Exchange and the Washington, Custis-Lee Enslaved Remembrance Society. She gives lectures and workshops on history and healing.

CHRONOLOGY

1607 English colonists arrive in Virginia.

1619 First African people brought to Virginia as slaves. By the late 1600s, race-based slavery is firmly rooted in the British colonies in North America.

FEBRUARY 22, 1732 George Washington is born to Augustine Washington and Mary Ball Washington at Pope's Creek Farm in Westmoreland County, Virginia.

1738 Washington family moves to Ferry Farm plantation near Fredericksburg, Virginia.

1743 Augustine Washington dies, leaving most of his property to George's older half brothers. George inherits Ferry Farm and 10 enslaved people.

1752 George's half-brother Lawrence Washington dies. George Washington receives an officer's commission in the Virginia militia.

1754 George Washington inherits Mount Vernon and a share of its resident slaves from Lawrence's estate.

1758 George Washington retires from the military, after being elected to the Virginia House of Burgesses.

1759 Washington weds Martha Dandridge Custis, who brings 85 slaves to the marriage.

1759-1775 Washington devotes himself to expanding Mount Vernon and turning it into a profitable, self-sufficient plantation. During this time he buys more than 60 slaves.

1768 William and Frank Lee are purchased by Washington and brought to Mount Vernon.

1773 Patsy Custis, Martha's daughter, dies at age 17.

1775-1783 Washington takes command of the Continental Army and leads the battle for freedom from Great Britain in the Revolutionary War. William Lee accompanies him throughout the struggle.

1781 Jacky Custis, Martha's son, dies at age 27, leaving four children. The two youngest, Nelly (Eleanor Parke Custis) and Washy (George Washington Parke Custis) are informally adopted by the Washingtons.

1783-1789 Washington returns to Mount Vernon and resumes the management of his various enterprises.

1786 Washington conducts the first complete census of Mount Vernon slaves and lists 216 men, women, and children. Of them, 105 are dower slaves belonging to the estate of Martha Washington's first husband, Daniel Parke Custis.

1789-1797 Washington is inaugurated as the first President of the United States in April 1789 and serves two terms. He resides first in New York and then in Philadelphia during his years in office.

MARCH 1797 Washington retires to Mount Vernon.

JULY 1799 Washington drafts a new will freeing his slaves.

DECEMBER 14, 1799 George Washington dies at age 67.

JANUARY 1, 1801 George Washington's 123 slaves are emancipated by Martha Washington.

MAY 22, 1802 Martha Washington dies at age 70. Her dower slaves are divided among her four grandchildren.

BIBLIOGRAPHY

PRIMARY SOURCE MATERIAL

The Papers of George Washington, Digital Edition. Edited by Theodore J. Crackel et al., University of Virginia Press, 2009.

Mount Vernon Guest Version: http://www .mountvernon.org/educational-resources/ library/research-databases. This digital archive contains Washington's diaries, letters, and papers, as well as letters written to him.

George Washington Papers at the Library of Congress, 1741-1799. Online at http:// memory.loc.gov/ammem/gwhtml. The largest collection of original Washington documents in the world. Includes letters, diaries, journals, financial account books, military records, reports, and notes.

Experiencing Mount Vernon: Eyewitness Accounts 1784-1865. Edited by Jean B. Lee. Charlottesville: University of Virginia Press, 2006.

Recollections and Private Memoirs of Washington. By George Washington Parke Custis. Philadelphia: William Flint, c. 1859.

BOOKS AND ARTICLES

Brady, Patricia. *Martha Washington: An American Life.* New York: Penguin Books, 2005.

Chernow, Ron. *Washington: A Life.* New York: Penguin Press, 2010.

Dalzell, Robert F., Jr., and Lee Dalzell. *George Washington's Mount Vernon: At Home in Revolutionary America.* New York: Oxford University Press, 1998.

Ellis, Joseph J. *His Excellency: George Washington.* New York: Vintage Books, 2004.

Freeman, Douglas S. *George Washington: A Biography,* volumes 2 and 3. New York: Charles Scribner's Sons, 1951.

Henriques, Peter R. *Realistic Visionary: A Portrait of George Washington.* Charlottesville: University of Virginia Press, 2006.

Hirschfeld, Fritz. *George Washington and Slavery: A Documentary Portrayal.* Columbia, MO: University of Missouri Press, 1997.

Horton, James Oliver, and Lois E. Horton. *Slavery and the Making of America.* New York: Oxford University Press, 2005.

"Information on Mount Vernon Slaves Who Died, Were Sold, or Escaped Prior to 1799." Compiled by Mary V. Thompson, 2005-2009. Mount Vernon Ladies' Association (MVLA).

McLeod, Stephen A., editor. *Dining With the Washingtons: Historic Recipes, Entertainment, and Hospitality From Mount Vernon.* Mount Vernon, VA: MVLA, 2011.

Morgan, Edmund S. *American Slavery, American Freedom: The Ordeal of Colonial Virginia.* New York: W. W. Norton & Company, 1975.

Morgan, Philip D. "To Get Quit of Negroes: George Washington and Slavery." Article presented as the Journal of American Studies Lecture at the British Association for American Studies Annual Conference, in April 2004; viewed on the Internet.

"Slavery at Mount Vernon." *Footsteps* maga- zine. Cobblestone Publications, November/ December 2000.

"Slaves at Mount Vernon in 1799: Slaves on the Dogue Run Farm-1799; Slaves Living on the Union Farm-1799; Slaves on the Mansion House Farm-1799; Slaves on the Muddy Hole Farm-1799; Slaves on the River Farm-1799." Compiled by Mary V. Thompson, 1995-2009. MVLA.

Schwarz, Philip J., editor. *Slavery at the Home of George Washington.* Mount Vernon, VA: MVLA, 2001.

Thompson, Mary V. "Different People, Different Stories." Presentation at a symposium entitled "George Washington and Slavery," Nov. 3, 2001; revised Nov. 2006. Mount Vernon Web site.

--------. *"In the Hands of a Good Providence": Religion in the Life of George Washington.* Charlottesville: University of Virginia Press, 2008.

--------. "The Lives of Enslaved Workers on George Washington's Outlying Farms." Presentation to the Neighborhood Friends of Mount Vernon, June 16, 1999. Mount Vernon Web site.

--------. "A Mean Pallet: The Slave Quarters at Mount Vernon." Unpublished research report. Typescript at Mount Vernon Library.

--------. "The Only Unavoidable Subject of Regret." Presentation to symposium "George Washington and Alexandria, Virginia: Ties That Bind," Feb. 20, 1999, updated Aug. 27, 2003. Typescript at Mount Vernon Library.

--------. "The Private Lives of Washington's Slaves." Excerpt from Virginia Calvacade, Volume 48, viewed at http://www.pbs.org/ wgbh/pages/frontline/shows/jefferson/video/ lives.html.

--------. "And Procure for Themselves a Few Amenities." Presentation to the Decorative Arts Symposium, November 9, 2006. Mount Vernon Web site.

Twohig, Dorothy. "That Species of Property: Washington's Role in the Controversy Over Slavery," in *George Washington Reconsidered.* Edited by Don Higginbotham. Pages 114-138. Charlottesville: University of Virginia Press, 2001.

Wiencek, Henry. *An Imperfect God: George Washington, His Slaves, and the Creation of America.* New York: Farrar, Straus and Giroux, 2003.

WEB SITES

George Washington's Mount Vernon Estate, Museum & Gardens. www.mountvernon .org. Full of information and images about our first President and the home he loved. Click "Meet George Washington" for links to biog- raphies, time lines, and more. See "Educational Resources" for sections for students and teachers.

The Papers of George Washington. http:// gwpapers.virginia.edu/index.html. Contains articles on Washington and slavery, Washington's will, and other topics; copies of slave lists and maps drawn up by Washington.

Slavery and the Making of America. http:// www.pbs.org/wnet/slavery/index.html. Companion Web site to the PBS documentary of the same name.

SOURCES

In order to help readers understand quotes from the 18th century, I have corrected nonstandard spellings and punctuation. Quotes are taken from the following sources, which are fully cited in the Bibliography. Whenever possible I have also included primary source information.

CHAPTER 1: A SHORT-LIVED CHILDHOOD
Page 10: The Papers of George Washington, Digital Edition (PGWDE); Page 11: "I thought I saw . . ." William Pearce to George Washington (GW), 19 Oct. 1793, in Dalzell, p. 137; Pages 11-12: "There are a great . . . have always been forbid . . ." DWTW to William Pearce, 27 Oct. 1793, in Dalzell, p. 137; Page 12: "a playground . . ." Diary of My Travels in America: Louis-Philippe, King of France (DMTALP), in Lee, p. 67; Page 13: "they may not be . . ." GW to William Pearce, 27 Oct. 1793, in Dalzell, p. 137; "So soon as they . . ." GW to William Stuart, Hyland Crow, and Henry McKay, 14 July 1793, in Dalzell, p. 138; "breaking limbs . . ." GW to William Pearce, 22 Dec. 1793, PGWDE.

FRANK LEE
Page 15: "The dishes . . ." Dining With the Washingtons (DWTW) p. 28; "make all the others . . ." DWTW, p. 75; "politeness and kindness" Slaves at Mount Vernon in 1799: Slaves on the Mansion House Farm-1799 (SMV-MHF 1799), p. 16; "most polite . . ." DWTW, p. 53; "ruined by idleness" GW to Anthony Whitting, 9 Dec. 1792, PGWDE.

CHAPTER 2: BUILDING A PLANTATION
Page 16: PGWDE; Page 19: GW to Daniel Jenifer Adams, 20 July 1772, in Wiencek, p. 120-121; Page 20: "healthy, strong . . ." GW to Joseph Thompson, 2 July 1766, in Chernow, p. 117; Page 21: "a Negro Girl named Sukey . . ." Wiencek, p. 181; "that my people . . ." GW to John Fairfax, 1 Jan. 1789, in Chernow, p. 30; Page 22: "the general's house servants . . ." DMTALP, in Lee, p. 68; "locked fast . . ." GW to Henry Knox, 5 Feb. 1788, in Chernow, p. 496; GW diary entry, 3 Jan. 1788, in Chernow, p. 496; "to feed and clothe . . . ought to render" GW to James Anderson, 20 Feb. 1797, in Henriques, p. 148; "people, with their blankets . . ." GW, River Farm plans, 10 Dec. 1799, in Thompson, "A Mean Pallet," p. 22.

DAVY
Page 23: "his business as well . . . insufferable conduct" GW to William Pearce, 18 Dec. 1793; "inattention and carelessness" GW to Anthony Whitting, 19 May 1793; "seems to consider a Negro . . ." GW to William Pearce, 10 May 1795; "knows the state . . ." GW to William Stuart, Hyland Crow, and Henry McKay, 14 July 1793, all in Thompson, "Lives of Enslaved Workers," p. 14-16; "Davy's lost lambs . . ." GW to William Pearce, 5 July 1795, in Dalzell, p. 267 note 34; "several of them would often . . ." GW to Anthony Whitting, 26 May 1793, PGWDE; "that house of . . ." Anthony Whitting to GW, 16 Jan. 1793, in Thompson, "Lives of Enslaved Workers," p. 11.

CHAPTER 3: PRIVATE LIVES
Page 24: PGWDE; Page 26: "they appear to live . . ." GW to Lund Washington (LW), 18 Feb. 1788, in Schwarz, p. 81; "very sorry . . ." LW to GW, 4 Mar. 1778, PGWDE; "In order to gratify" GW to Lund Washington, 3 Apr. 1779; "never failed . . ." GW to Anthony Whitting, 9 Dec. 1792, SMV-MHF 1799; "duties of . . ." GW to William Pearce, 18 May 1794, in Hirschfeld, p. 43; Page 27: "be particularly attentive . . ." GW to Anthony Whitting, 14 Oct. 1792, in Hirschfeld, p. 40; Page 28: "I see by . . ." GW to William Pearce, 21 Feb. 1796, in Thompson, "And Procure for Themselves a Few Amenities," p. 7; "for taking up Caesar . . ." GW, 7 Apr. 1798, Cash Memoranda, in Slaves Living on the Union Farm-1799 (SLUF-1799), p. 19; Page 29: "tell of days . . ." Recollections and Private Memoirs of Washington (RPMW) by George Washington Parke Custis, p. 93; "a bright mahogany . . ." An Old Citizen of Fairfax County, "Mount Vernon Reminiscences," Alexandria Gazette, 18 Jan. 1876, in Thompson, "Different People," p. 3; "the son of a king" Alexandria Gazette, 18 Jan. 1876, in Thompson, "Different People," p. 4; "great Newfoundland" RPMW, p. 457, in SMV-MHF 1799, p. 50; Page 30: "seine haulers . . ." GW Fishery Account, 15 Mar. 1798, in Thompson, "Procure for Themselves," p. 3; "It is not my wish . . ." GW to Anthony Whitting, 26 May 1793, PGWDE.

HERCULES
Page 31: "new habitation . . . dirty figures . . ." GW to Tobias Lear, 9 Sept. 1790, Information on MV Slaves Who Died, Were Sold, or Escaped Prior to 1799 (IMVSWD), p. 21; "gloried in . . . pleasing manner" RPMW, p. 422-423, in IMVSWD, p. 32; "running off . . ." LW to George Lewis, 13 Nov. 1797, in Hirschfeld, p. 15; "Oh! Sir . . ." DMTALP, in Lee, p. 68.

CHAPTER 4: RESISTANCE AND CONTROL
Page 32: PGWDE; Page 33: "every laborer . . ." GW to John Fairfax, 1 Jan. 1789, PGWDE; "yellowish complexion . . . judicious Negro" Maryland Gazette advertisement, August 1761, PGWDE; Page 34: "within a few . . ." GW diary entry, 30 Jan. 1760, in Wiencek, p. 100; "went off without . . ." Maryland Gazette advertisement, August 1761, PGWDE; Page 35: "Nothing pleases me better . . ." GW to William Pearce, 6 Oct. 1793, in Chernow, p. 119; "keep everyone . . ." GW to Anthony Whitting, 14 Oct. 1792, in Chernow, p. 640; "spirit of thieving . . ." GW to Anthony Whitting, 19 May 1793, PGWDE; "I cannot conceive . . ." GW to Anthony Whitting, 3 Feb. 1793, in Hirschfeld, p. 35; "underling shop keepers . . ." GW to William Pearce, 1 June 1794, in Hirschfeld, p. 35; Page 35-36: "frolicking at the . . ." GW to Anthony Whitting, 2 Dec. 1792, in Chernow, p. 461; Page 37: "I have minded 'em . . ." Humphrey Knight to GW, 2 Sept. 1758, in Dalzell, p. 141; Page 38: "all irregularities . . ." GW to Anthony Whitting, 5 May 1793, in Chernow, p. 113; "that if his pride . . ." GW to Anthony Whitting, 19 May 1793, in Hirschfeld, p. 36; "He, his father . . ." GW to Anthony Whitting, 16 March 1793, in Hirschfeld, p. 37.

CHARLOTTE
Page 39: "flog . . . contemptuous" Charles MacIver to GW, 17 June 1786, in Thompson, "Different People," p. 26; "a very good whipping . . . skin her back" Anthony Whitting to GW, 16 Jan. 1793, PGWDE; "Your treatment of . . ." GW to Anthony Whitting, 20 Jan. 1793, in Thompson, "Different People," p. 28; "drank freely . . ." GW to William Pearce, 18 Dec. 1793, in Thompson, "Different People," p. 28; "be placed . . ." GW to Anthony Whitting, 23 Dec. 1792, PGWDE.

CHAPTER 5: A CHANGE OF HEART
Page 40: PGWDE; Page 41: "neither Negroes . . ." GW General Orders, 12 Nov. 1775, in Wiencek, p. 202: "It has been represented . . ." GW to John Hancock, 31 Dec. 1775, PGWDE; Page 42: "You never see . . ." Wiencek, p. 191; "elegant lines . . ." GW to Phillis Wheatley, 28 Feb. 1776, in Wiencek, p. 213; Page 43, "very courteous . . ." Chernow, p. 220; "so attached . . ." Lund Washington to GW, 3 Dec. 1775, PGWDE; "every day . . . more and more . . ." GW to Lund Washington, 15 Aug. 1778, in Hirschfeld, p. 28; "without her consent" Lund Washington to GW, 8 Apr. 1778, in Hirschfeld, p. 27; Page 44: "I would never . . ." Chernow, p. 485; "there is not a man . . ." GW to Robert Morris, 12 Apr. 1786, in Thompson, "The Only Unavoidable . . ." p. 11; "to possess another . . . slow sure . . ." GW to John Francis Mercer, 9 Sept. 1786, in Chernow, p. 490; Page 45, "I shall frankly . . ." GW to Alexander Spotswood, 23 Nov. 1794, in Henriques, p. 162; "the servants of the . . ." Wiencek, p. 313; Page 46: "would be benefited . . ." GW to Tobias Lear, 12 Apr. 1791, in Wiencek, p. 316; "growing more . . ." GW to Alexander Spotswood, 14 Sept. 1798, in Chernow, p. 800.

WILLIAM LEE
Page 47: "best horseman . . ." Thomas Jefferson to Dr. Walter Jones, 2 Jan. 1814, in Hirschfeld, p. 98; "refuse [Lee's] request . . ." GW to Clement Biddle, 28 July 1784, in Hirschfeld, p. 106.

CHAPTER 6: LIBERTY AT LAST
Page 48: PGWDE; Page 49: "the ingratitude . . ." GW to the Secretary of the Treasury, 1 Sept. 1796, in Chernow, p. 761; "The unfortunate condition . . ." comment by GW, recorded by his former secretary David Humphries, in Thompson, "In the Hands of a Good Providence," p. 90; "they hoped . . ." DMTALP, in Lee, p. 68; "liberate a certain . . ." GW to Tobias Lear, 6 May 1794, in Wiencek, p. 274; Page 50, "It is demonstratively . . ." GW to Robert Lewis, 17 Aug. 1799, in Ellis, p. 258; "that no reproach . . ." GW to James McHenry, 25 March 1799, in Chernow, p. 801; "slow poison . . ." George Mason's Views on Slavery, Gunston Hall Web site, www.gunstonhall.org; "abominable crime" Thomas Jefferson and Slavery, Monticello Web site, www.monticello. org; "most oppressive . . ." from a speech by James Madison at the Constitutional Convention, June 1787, Montpelier Web site, www.montpelier. org; Page 51: George Washington's Last Will and Testament, 9 July 1799, PGWDE.

CHRISTOPHER SHEELS
Page 53: "nothing short . . ." letter of GW to Tobias Lear, 11 Aug. 1793, in Hirschfeld, p. 107; "celebrated for curing . . ." SMV-MHF 1799, p. 30; "pay whatever . . ." GW to William Stoy, 14 Oct. 1797, PGWDE; "pleasure in informing . . ." GW to George Washington Lafayette, 5 Dec. 1797, in SMV-MHF 1799, p. 30; "a mulatto girl . . ." GW to Roger West, 19 Sept. 1799, in SMV-MHF 1799, p. 30.

EPILOGUE
Page 54: "she did not feel . . ." Abigail Adams to her sister Mary, 21 Dec. 1800, in Hirschfeld, p. 214; "the most respectable . . ." 1876 correspondent in the Alexandria Gazette, in SMV-MHF 1799, p. 57.

INDEX

DEDICATION

For my family, all the Fergusons and Hardins and Delanos and Batemans, with love
—MFD

For my sister, Kim, and her boys, Samuel & Jakey
—LE

PREPARED BY THE BOOK DIVISION

Melina Gerosa Bellows, *Executive Vice President; Chief Creative Officer, Books, Kids, and Family;* Hector Sierra, *Senior Vice President and General Manager;* Nancy Laties Feresten, *Senior Vice President, Kids Publishing and Media;* Jonathan Halling, *Design Director, Books and Children's Publishing;* Jay Sumner, *Director of Photography, Children's Publishing;* Jennifer Emmett, *Vice President, Editorial Director, Children's Books;* Eva Absher-Schantz, *Design Director, Kids Publishing and Media;* Carl Mehler, *Director of Maps;* R. Gary Colbert, *Production Director;* Jennifer A. Thornton, *Director of Managing Editorial*

STAFF FOR THIS BOOK

Jennifer Emmett, *Project Editor;* James Hiscott, Jr., *Art Director/Designer;* Lori Epstein, *Senior Illustrations Editor;* Kate Olesin, *Associate Editor;* Kathryn Robbins, *Design Production Assistant;* Hillary Moloney, *Illustrations Assistant;* Gregory Ugiansky, *Map Production;* Grace Hill, *Associate Managing Editor;* Joan Gossett, *Production Editor;* Lewis R. Bassford, *Production Manager;* Susan Borke, *Legal and Business Affairs*

MANUFACTURING AND QUALITY MANAGEMENT

Phillip L. Schlosser, *Senior Vice President;* Chris Brown, *Vice President, Book Manufacturing;* George Bounelis, *Vice President, Production Services;* Rachel Faulise, Nicole Elliott, and Robert L. Barr, *Managers*

ILLUSTRATION CREDITS

All photography by Lori Epstein unless otherwise noted below:

Cover, North Wind Picture Archives/Alamy; cover (inset), White House Historical Association; cover (inset), SVLuma/Shutterstock; front endpaper, Susan Law Cain/Shutterstock; back endpaper, photography by Mark Gulezian/QuickSilver Photographers LLC/courtesy Fairfax County Court; 5, White House Historical Association; 5, SVLuma/Shutterstock; 6-7, Courtesy of Mount Vernon Ladies' Association; 10, Courtesy of Mount Vernon Ladies' Association; 14 (top), Courtesy of Mount Vernon Ladies' Association; 14 (bottom), The Bridgeman Art Library/Getty Images; 15, Sketch of a group for a drawing of Mount Vernon. Not dated. Work on paper by Benjamin Henry Latrobe. Courtesy of the Maryland Historical Society; 17, Courtesy of Mount Vernon Ladies' Association; 18 (top), Courtesy of Mount Vernon Ladies' Association; 19, Michael Deas; 20, Courtesy of Mount Vernon Ladies' Association; 22 (top), Courtesy of Mount Vernon Ladies' Association; 24, Courtesy of Mount Vernon Ladies' Association; 29, Sora DeVore; 31, © Museo Thyssen-Bornemisza, Madrid; 32, Courtesy of Mount Vernon Ladies' Association; 35, National Geographic Digital Motion; 38, © 2005 The Colonial Williamsburg Foundation; 39, An Overseer Doing his Duty near Fredericksburg, Virginia. Ca. 1798. Work on paper by Benjamin Henry Latrobe. Courtesy Maryland Historical Society; 40, Undercover History: The Real George Washington/Nicole Teusch/NGT; 42, Washington and Lafayette at Valley Forge/painting by Dunsmore/UIG via Getty Images; 43, Anonymous (often attributed to Scipio Moorhead)/Photograph courtesy of Babcock Galleries, New York; 44, Courtesy of Mount Vernon Ladies' Association; 45, Undercover History: The Real George Washington/Tim Fenoglio/NGT; 47, Courtesy of Mount Vernon Ladies' Association; 48, Edward Savage, The Washington Family,1789-1796, Andrew W. Mellon Collection/Image Courtesy National Gallery of Art; 50 (top), White House Historical Association; 50 (center), Library of Congress; 50 (bottom), White House Historical Association; 51, Courtesy of Mount Vernon Ladies' Association; 52, photography by Mark Gulezian/QuickSilver Photographers LLC/courtesy Fairfax County Court; 53, Edward Savage, The Washington Family,1789-1796, Andrew W. Mellon Collection/Image Courtesy National Gallery of Art; 55 (top), Courtesy of Mount Vernon Ladies' Association; 55 (bottom), photography by Mark Gulezian/QuickSilver Photographers LLC/courtesy Fairfax County Court

FRONT COVER: A 19th-century print depicts an idyllic view of George Washington and his African-American slaves at Mount Vernon. The two white children probably represent Washington's step-grandchildren.
BACK COVER: A costumed interpreter portraying an 18th-century enslaved worker walks near the sixteen-sided barn at Mount Vernon.
FRONT ENDPAPER: The United States Declaration of Independence
BACK ENDPAPER: George Washington's Last Will and Testament
HALF TITLE AND FRONT COVER INSET: Hand-tinted engraving of George Washington based on a 1796 portrait by Gilbert Stuart

For more information, please call 1-800-NGS LINE (647-5463) or write to the following address:

National Geographic Society
1145 17th Street N.W.
Washington, D.C. 20036-4688 U.S.A.

Visit us online at nationalgeographic.com/books

For librarians and teachers:
ngchildrensbooks.org

More for kids from National Geographic:
kids.nationalgeographic.com

For information about special discounts for bulk purchases, please contact National Geographic Books Special Sales: ngspecsales@ngs.org

For rights or permissions inquiries, please contact National Geographic Books Subsidiary Rights: ngbookrights@ngs.org

Book design by James Hiscott, Jr.
Text is in Adobe Jenson Pro; Display text in Chase and Battery Park; Dingbats in Type Embellishments Two.

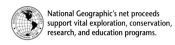

LIBRARY OF CONGRESS CATALOGING-IN-PUBLICATION DATA

Master George's People.
Delano, Marfe Ferguson.
Master George's people : George Washington, his slaves, and his revolutionary transformation / By Marfe Ferguson Delano.
   pages cm
Includes bibliographical references and index.
ISBN 978-1-4263-0759-1 (hardcover : alk. paper) -- ISBN 978-1-4263-0760-7 (library binding : alk. paper)
1. Washington, George, 1732-1799--Relations with slaves. 2. Slaves--Virginia--Mount Vernon (Estate) 3. Slavery--Virginia--Mount Vernon (Estate) 4. Mount Vernon (Va. : Estate)--Race relations. I. Title.
E312.17.D38 2013
973.4'1092--dc23
[B]
                         2012024295

Printed in China
12/CCOS/1

In the name of God amen

I George Washing[ton] of Mount Vernon — a citi[zen of] the United States, — and lately Pr[esi]dent of the same, do make, orda[in] and declare this Instrument; [which] is written with my own hand, [and] every page there[of] subscribed [with] my name, to be my last Will & [Tes]tament, revoking all other[s].

[Im]primus. All m[y de]bts, of which there are but few, and [none of] magnitude are to be punctu[ally] and speedily paid — and the Legaci[es her]einafter bequeathed, are to be disc[ha]rged as soon as cir[cum]stances will [pe]rmit, and in the — manner directe[d].

[It]em. To my dear[ly] loved wife Mar[]tha Washington [I] give and bequeath the use, profit [and] benefit of my whole Estate, real and [per]sonal; for the term of her natural li[fe] — except such parts thereof as are s[pec]ifically disposed of hereafter: — [my] ... lot in the Town of Ale[xandria] Pitt & Cameron ... her heirs forev[er]